A SAINT'S JOURNEY
on the
NARROW PATH

Other Books by Clark Rich Burbidge

Fiction: Gold Medal Award-Winning Young Adult Series:

StarPassage: Book One – The Relic
StarPassage: Book Two – Heroes and Martyrs
StarPassage: Book Three – Honor and Mercy
StarPassage: Book Four – Cyber Plague

Fiction: Gold Medal Award-Winning Young Adult / Middle Reader Trilogy:

Giants in the Land: Book One – The Way of Things
Giants in the Land: Book Two – The Prodigals
Giants in the Land: Book Three – The Cavern of Promise

Fiction: Gold Medal Award-Winning Family Christmas Picture Book:

A Piece of Silver: A Story of Christ

Fiction: Gold Medal Award-Winning Juvenile Picture Books:

Brave Howie and the Terrible Giant
Brave Howie and the Great Whisker Mystery

Nonfiction:

Life on the Narrow Path:
A Mountain Biker's Guide to Spiritual Growth in Troubled Times

Gold Medal Award-Winning Family Book with Leah D. Burbidge:

Living in the Family Blender: 10 Principles of a Successful Blended Family

Websites:
www.starpassagebook.com
www.giantsinthelandbook.com
www.apieceofsilver.com

A SAINT'S JOURNEY
on the
NARROW PATH

CLARK RICH BURBIDGE

CFI
An imprint of Cedar Fort, Inc.
Springville, Utah

© 2025 Clark Rich Burbidge
All rights reserved.

No part of this book may be reproduced in any form whatsoever, whether by graphic, visual, electronic, film, microfilm, tape recording, or any other means, without prior written permission of the publisher, except in the case of brief passages embodied in critical reviews and articles.

This is not an official publication of The Church of Jesus Christ of Latter-day Saints. The opinions and views expressed herein belong solely to the author and do not necessarily represent the opinions or views of Cedar Fort, Inc. Permission for the use of sources, graphics, and photos is also solely the responsibility of the author.

Paperback ISBN 13: 978-1-4621-4924-7
eBook ISBN 13: 978-1-4621-4925-4

Published by CFI, an imprint of Cedar Fort, Inc.
2373 W. 700 S., Suite 100, Springville, UT 84663
Distributed by Cedar Fort, Inc., www.cedarfort.com

Library of Congress Cataloging Number: 2024951892

Cover design by Shawnda Craig
Cover design © 2025 Cedar Fort, Inc.
Edited and Typeset by Liz Kazandzhy

Printed in the United States of America

10 9 8 7 6 5 4 3 2 1

Printed on acid-free paper

For teens and young adults. Your life matters.
Get in the arena and fight. Make yours count.

Contents

Preface: The Last Deep Secret We All Keep ix

Introduction xvii

1 Dwelling on Obstacles 1

2 Focusing Ahead 7

3 Preparation and Anticipation 13

4 Riding with a Guide and Knowing the Trail 23

5 Momentum and Practice 31

6 Awareness and Utilizing Gifts 39

7 Sometimes You Hit the Rock Anyway 47

8 Map Reading: The Big Picture 61

9 A Sense of Humor and a Good Pace 73

10 Shepherding: Riding with Others 81

11 Knowing Your Personal Limits 91

12 Respecting the Trail 97

13 Picking the Right Line 107

14 The Downhill Ride 115

15 Why Me? 125

16 It's a Beautiful Day for a Ride 137

Epilogue: How to Identify a Mountain Biker 143

Acknowledgments 151

About the Author 155

Preface: The Last Deep Secret We All Keep

THIS IS NOT REALLY A BOOK ABOUT BIKING, AND YET IT'S VERY MUCH about mountain biking, road biking, and life. During my tens of thousands of miles of traveling on mountain and road rides, I have had time to think. Sometimes the thoughts are random; other times they're about difficult issues at work or dilemmas in dealing with family matters. New insights and even revelation are also part of many rides. However, it is not uncommon for me to contemplate principles of eternity and faith. During such thoughtful moments, I have found numerous parallels between (1) negotiating the narrow mountain single track or surviving the unexpected moments of road rides and (2) dealing with life's similar strait gate and narrow path (see Matthew 7:13–14; Luke 13:24; 2 Nephi 33:9). It is these lessons—absorbed "line upon line, precept upon precept" (2 Nephi 28:30) over years of participation in life—that I hope you will find in this guide. Learn these principles well. They will keep you safe and allow you to more fully enjoy your ride on both paths.

The thing that brings freedom is not unrestricted activity to do whatever you want, whenever you want, with no limits. That, in fact, brings chaos, one of Satan's favorite tools for the prideful or narcissistic.

Rather, the gift of true freedom is realized through the careful focus and learning of applicable principles, rules, skills, and mechanics of any endeavor, along with much real-life practice. As with mountain biking, using just one or two of these principles helps, but it is the mastery and effective employment of all the principles in concert that will make your experience along the narrow path more satisfying and successful.

Life Can Change in an Instant

I was diagnosed with degenerative arthritis in both my hips at the age of thirty-seven in 1992. It was a shock for someone who had been a two-sport varsity athlete in high school and college and continued to live a very active life. Was the cause genetic or just some unfortunate twist of fate? Maybe it was from overuse, from some untreated and unremembered injury of the past, or from that year I moved three times, carrying most of the items myself for two of those moves. Twenty-six years later, no one had been able to determine the cause. It was discouraging not to know, but in life, we often don't get easy answers to our "Why?" questions. In fact, life tends not to slow down for such moments; the steep climbs seem to come without regard for our need to catch our breath. On the other hand, we must recognize and efficiently utilize the easier stretches whenever they occur. This allows us to build momentum and reserve our strength for the tough climbs that surely will continue to loom before us, perhaps just around the next bend.

It has gradually dawned on me that discovering the reasons we face individual challenges does not matter very much. What does matter is accepting responsibility for where we are and how we manage the obstacles we come upon. God has a plan for us to return to His presence. It seems that our individual plan of salvation includes with it some personally tailored challenges that can be daunting. Yet it is these individual trials, if faced with courage and faith, that first build and then strengthen the foundation of our spiritual growth and our ability to endure greater and greater challenges as we continue to press forward.

PREFACE: THE LAST DEEP SECRET WE ALL KEEP

This is what John the Revelator referred to as "overcoming" (see Revelation 2 and 3). It is at the very heart of the Lord's counsel, given through Isaiah and Nephi, that we will receive "line upon line, precept upon precept, here a little and there a little; and blessed are those who hearken unto my precepts, and lend an ear unto my counsel, for they shall learn wisdom; for unto him that receiveth I will give more" (1 Nephi 28:30)—that we might be properly instructed as we are able to appreciate it. Notice that this growth occurs little by little based on our willingness to hear, learn, and do His will (see Isaiah 28:14; Mark 4:24; Luke 6:49; James 1:22). As we make correct choices and "overcome," setbacks can and do provide critical wisdom and the perspective necessary to drive our roots deep into good ground. This, combined with an attitude of ongoing nourishment through consistent and faithful "doing," allows the earth in which we are planted to become rich, secure, and productive. The blessing to those who diligently persevere, as the Savior stated, is that the resulting faith produces good fruit (see Matthew 7:16–20; Alma 32:41–42). In fact, the Savior went on to point out that it is the resulting "good treasure of [our] heart" (Matthew 12:35) that brings forth these good fruits.

My original medical diagnosis advised that I could continue with my high-impact activities—soccer, running, basketball, softball, and skiing/jumping—or I could look to find new, lower-impact pastimes like biking and swimming. If I chose poorly, I was told to expect a hip replacement within three to five years with a second replacement ten years after that and then, after the second one wore out, a life in a wheelchair or some other severely limited state.

Of course, the technology and prognosis for hip replacements changed during the ensuing twenty-six years, but at the time, the downside was sobering. If I chose wisely, the doctor explained, any operation could be put off for years, depending on how I felt. No promises, of course, but there was hope, and hope can be a powerful motivator for positive change. Paul knew well the great power of hope grounded in faith: "[May] the God of hope fill you with all joy and peace in believing, that ye may abound in hope, through the power of the Holy Ghost" (Romans 15:13), and "he that ploweth should plow in hope; and that he that thresheth in hope should be partaker of his hope" (1 Corinthians 9:10). To the Hebrews, Paul referred to hope as "an anchor of the soul" (Hebrews 6:19). Ether also spoke of this great anchor when he said, "Whoso believeth in God might with surety hope for a better world, yea, even a place at the right hand of God, which hope cometh of faith, maketh an anchor to the souls of men, which would make them sure and steadfast" (Ether 12:4).

As you might expect, I did my best to use this anchor of my soul and choose wisely. I took up mountain biking and was fortunate to be living at the mouth of a canyon with one of the state's greatest mountain bike trails. Because of the ideal location, I also discovered many who already enjoyed the activity and were glad to show me the ropes. Some would become lifelong friends and riding buddies. I also did other things like taking supplements to build up my hips, keeping my weight down, and engaging in activities that have been rigorous but lower-impact. While I haven't been the perfect example of diet or weight management and sometimes have participated in some high-impact activities with my friends, children, and grandchildren, the results of these adjustments were satisfying. For many years, my joints felt better than they had since my mid-thirties, and as an added bonus, I learned some important lessons about spiritual growth and finding happiness along the way in spite of continuing challenges.

The Last Secret

In the life and growth of every person, there is that one last thing that they somehow cannot bring themselves to confess. That last fear, or failing, is often buried so deep that they refuse to acknowledge it, even to themselves. But to be completely free and unburdened, it must eventually be faced. My acknowledgment and self-confession came in 2018. Over the years, I had been slowly losing flexibility. I was walking slower and could barely bend over. Putting my socks on had become a real trick. But I continued to ignore it because I was not in pain most of the time. Sure, I could no longer sleep on my side because of the pain, and hiking without two walking sticks was not possible, but I could still ride—although I slid from side to side on the seat because my hips would not bend quite enough to pedal.

My wife Leah convinced me to get an appointment with the orthopedist, and unbeknownst to me, my period of denial was over. I finally allowed an orthopedic surgeon to x-ray my hips in May 2018, and sobering news resulted. I was informed that both hip joints essentially no longer existed. They were fused to my pelvis, and the bending that was occurring was not my hip but rather my pelvis. This explained why I felt a slow bending and unbending whenever I sat down or stood up. The doctor calmly described the risk that one day I would be sitting down or getting up, riding or simply bending over, and my pelvis would snap. This would produce serious and possibly permanent and crippling problems.

I was stunned and humbled by the revelation and decided on the spot to have both hips replaced. The operations were set for June and July, four weeks apart. I spent the ensuing month researching recovery experiences and found them mostly encouraging. At one point, I even pulled up a YouTube video of a hip replacement operation and started watching it. I made it only about thirty seconds into the video before shutting it down—I didn't want to have that kind of detail in my head. I did end up watching it later after the surgeries, but at that earlier point in time, it wasn't wise.

Our plans to have the operations four weeks apart were blown up when my first hip operation was delayed two weeks due to an issue with the insurance approval. Instead, I ended up having both hips done during a two-week period from mid-June to early July of 2018. Both operations were successfully completed, although I advise a bit more time in between. I was awkwardly back on the stationary bike and elliptical machine within three days of my second hip replacement and then walking around the block, first with crutches and then without.

Biking again became my path to health and normal activity. Ten days into my recovery, I remember I tried riding around the block with one of my sons, Neil, jogging next to me. By the end of July, I was back to road biking a hundred miles per week, and I did my first mountain biking ride up the Mueller Park Trail before the end of October. My goal was to get at least one mountain bike ride in that fall, and I barely got it in.

In retrospect, I've learned that everyone, including myself, has that one thing in their life that's the last one that will ever be revealed, admitted to, or personally addressed. For me, it was an unwillingness to seriously consider, or even attempt to discover, the extent of my hip problems. Each of us is eventually forced by life to face such realities and their ramifications on us as well as those around us.

Part of our individual denial is always a denial regarding how serious the impact is on those around us. Facing the truth and taking concrete action to overcome it is not only healthy, but it is also a certain way to stop defining our lives by the past or by various burdens we have chosen to continue to carry. The adversary seeks to have us constantly and forever looking backward and wallowing in past mistakes or injustices. He would rather have us refuse to face those obstacles and have us forever define ourselves by our most harmful traits or secrets.

God Does Not Define Us by Our Past

God does not define us by our past, and we shouldn't either. He focuses on where we are and the direction we're headed. That is what should define us. The beauty of a personal and loving Heavenly Father is that He is willing to start with us wherever we are and take the next steps together. It makes no difference to Him how dark the place is in which we turn to Him. He will hear and respond.

I have chosen my experiences with mountain and road biking as the context in which to frame these soul-saving lessons learned. Such principles have been an important part of my ability to continue to "stand" (see 1 Corinthians 16:13) while enduring physical, family, financial, and spiritual challenges. Looking back, I cannot imagine anyone surviving such experiences intact, let alone myself. Yet somehow I'm here, still standing, having regained my range of motion and flexibility, active, happy, and spiritually progressing.

I am thankful to my Heavenly Father for always being there, for never pulling down the signposts, for placing wonderful individuals in my path at critical moments to strengthen me during times of extreme need, and for allowing me to feel the great personal love He has for each of His children, including me. I am grateful for my Savior, Jesus Christ, who took upon Him all our sins, disappointments, pains, wounds, injuries at the hands of others, and so much more that we might overcome during this life and return to live with our Father.

PREFACE: THE LAST DEEP SECRET WE ALL KEEP

I believe our part is to strive to do our best. This allows the Savior's atoning sacrifice to become effective in our lives through repenting, forgiving others, keeping our covenants, and hanging in there. By doing this, we begin to exclude from our hearts those things that canker and destroy while replacing them with those things that are lovely and of good report (see Philippians 4:8; Articles of Faith 1:13).

During the past thirty-two years the principles shared herein have strengthened me through illness, the passing of both my parents, personal and national economic crises, wars, rumors of wars, terrorism, life's storms, challenges in my children's lives, job and career changes, intense family difficulties and all their attendant burdens, and the many other stressful and discouraging experiences of which life seems to be so full.

STILL STANDING

Today I continue to literally stand straight and tall and ride about 120 miles per week. I only partly jokingly tell people that my new hips have taught me a part of the joy one might feel having their body resurrected—because my hips certainly feel forty years younger! The many gifts I celebrate include my beautiful wife and our blended family of ten children and thirteen grandchildren—they are examples of God returning twice our blessings as we continue faithful (see Job 42:10).

Looking back, I can see more clearly that overcoming much of the personal mountain range in which my climbs have taken place was only possible because I was being carried in my Savior's loving arms much of the way. It was a far greater challenge than I was capable of surmounting alone. In my mid-thirties, I thought I understood the Atonement well. What I did not perceive was that real understanding only begins with sincerely studying the writings of prophets and apostles. It then proceeds with the fervent prayer that only life's trials can produce, especially those that require patience and long-suffering to endure and overcome on God's time frame.

As we grow, the words of Isaiah regarding the mission and purpose of the Savior have new meaning: "Surely he hath borne our griefs, and carried our sorrows: yet we did esteem him stricken, smitten of

God, and afflicted. But he was wounded for our transgressions, he was bruised for our iniquities: the chastisement of our peace was upon him; and with his stripes we are healed" (Isaiah 53:4–5). Alma adds additional insight: "He will take upon him the pains and the sicknesses of his people . . . [and] their infirmities . . . that he may know according to the flesh how to succor his people according to their infirmities" (Alma 7:11–12). The Savior took upon Himself so much more than just our sins.

A common misunderstanding in reviewing Paul's writings to the Corinthians is that God will not tempt or place any burden upon us that is greater than we can bear. In fact, a more complete understanding of the scripture reinforces that this life will often place upon us burdens greater than we can bear. However, it also tells us that God will "make a way to escape, that ye may be able to bear it" (1 Corinthians 10:13). Numerous other references support the idea that this life and the tests we face are specifically designed to be more than we can bear *alone*. Yes, that is the key—we cannot bear these by ourselves, but we can bear all things if we look to our Father and our Savior and bear them together. The Lord can give us rest (see Matthew 11:28), make our burdens lighter (see Matthew 11:30), and share the bearing of burdens through others (see Galatians 6:2). Blindly attempting to forge on by ourselves, relying on our own strength, results in our body and soul eventually being crushed by the multiplying weight (see Proverbs 3:5–6; Romans 8:1; 2 Nephi 4:34; 2 Nephi 28:31). It is the difference between standing in the surf, allowing the waves to beat you down, and *using* the power of the waves, as surfers or boogie boarders do, to propel them to greater things.

While the details are personal, I don't believe I exaggerate much when I say that I understand some portion of what it is like to live through the first chapter of Job (see Job 1:13–22; 2:1–10). But happily, I have also had the pleasure to learn what the last chapter of Job feels like (see Job 42:12–15). I prefer the last chapter without question. Could I have appreciated the blessings and understood with my heart had I not experienced the earlier chapters as well? I think not.

Introduction

THE MOUNTAIN AND ROAD BIKING EXPERIENCES REFERENCED IN THIS book are primarily from my many rides on the Mueller Park Trail in Bountiful, Utah, and rides on the Legacy Trail in Davis County, Utah, from 1992 through 2024 unless otherwise specifically referenced.

The Mueller Park Trail is an approximately 3.5-mile single track from the trailhead, which is at about a 5,200-foot elevation, to Big Rock (also referred to as Elephant Rock), where there's a beautiful view and nowadays a bench, the result of some young man's Eagle Project. For those who don't know, a single track is a narrow, one-lane trail. By comparison, a double track is commonly a track made by a four-wheeled vehicle.

The trail continues another approximately 3.0 miles to the summit, called Rudy's Flats (elevation: about 7,100 feet), where many turn around and return down the Mueller Park side. The trail rises approximately 1,900 feet, the majority of which (about 1,100 feet) occurs from the trailhead to Big Rock. One can continue on approximately 3.0 more miles from Rudy's Flats down the North Canyon side and, using surfaced roads, complete a 12-mile loop back to the Mueller Park trailhead parking lot. In recent years, a new Shoreline Trail has been developed that runs basically from North Salt Lake City up to Farmington.

The trail can be busy on a Saturday or holiday, but it never feels crowded and is never a dull ride. It accommodates bikers, joggers, hikers, and the occasional horse or even motorcycle (although it's extremely narrow and doesn't comfortably fit the latter two). It is well maintained, although in the early spring, you should expect to find a tree or two that has fallen onto the trail during the winter. I have ridden this trail as many as eighty times per year in all conditions—from snow and ice in the early spring, through 100-plus-degree days in the summer, and as late as early December. In fact, in one particularly dry year, I was able to ride up to Big Rock every month of the year except January. While riding, you may come across a huge variety of animals—moose, deer, elk, porcupines, birds (including bald eagles and turkey vultures), numerous and various forest mammals, snakes (including the occasional rattlesnake), cougars, and many animals of the human and canine variety. It produces an atmosphere where every ride is a new adventure.

While my road rides have taken place in many locations and states, my primary references will be to rides on what is known as the Davis County Legacy Trail, which connects to the Jordan River Trail on the south end and runs at least to north Ogden. My rides on this trail generally include a 24-mile ride from my home to just north of Farmington Station and looping back, although some go as far as Kaysville and back, which is my 33-mile loop. Once per year, I'll be joined by family and friends for a ride that is as many miles as I am old in years. This past year was my 69-mile ride at 69 years old. That requires a ride from my home to Antelope Island in the middle of the Great Salt Lake and back.

These rides allow much time to contemplate life and its challenges. They also allow the quietude to boldly examine life's problems and find solutions. But mostly they allow one the opportunity to appreciate the beauty of God's creations while getting some solid exercise. *A Saint's Journey on the Narrow Path* does not include all the principles by which one may successfully participate in the activity. Every time I ride, I think of additional ways to make the experience more efficient and enjoyable. It's a learning process, and as you master principles,

INTRODUCTION

more and higher principles are revealed. This is the secret to experiencing real freedom. The same is true of spiritual growth. Certainly, this work does not pretend to present all the principles whereby one may grow closer to God and find true joy in this life. Like mountain biking itself, spiritual growth comes as an individualized process with new insights revealed along the way. I hope you enjoy these insights and find them helpful. I pray that as you make them part of your life, you will realize other insights as well.

1

Dwelling on Obstacles

MOUNTAIN BIKING REQUIRES A COMBINATION OF CONDITIONING, judgment, momentum, and balance. Biking on a narrow single track, which often has steep drop-offs just inches off the track, tests all these abilities often simultaneously. This particular narrow track ride is often made more technical by loose or fixed rocks and roots, several narrow bridges, and logs placed cross-trail to prevent erosion. These obstacles—along with hikers, dogs, joggers, and riders going both ways—require continuous vigilance.

The first true principle of mountain biking is not to dwell on the obstacles. This means that if there's something in the trail moving or stationary, loose or fixed, which your eyes or mind becomes focused on, your front tire will be drawn directly toward it. The experience can be particularly memorable if the fixation is the drop-off on the edge of the trail or a biker moving in the opposite direction. This means you hit what you stare at. And trust me, this is not a pleasant experience.

I remember following a twenty-something rider down two switchbacks near the bottom of the trail. Marking the inside of both these steep downhill turns are sturdy trees. In an effort to avoid the trail's edge as she attempted the downhill turn, she focused so hard on the inside of the switchbacks that she crashed, solidly impacting the tree trunks on both bends. She went over the handlebars both times into the tree. Following the first crash, I stopped to offer assistance and advice about this principle, but after the second one, she merely gave me an embarrassed look and waved me past. That's not something you see every day!

The result is often the same whether you have a lot of momentum or very little—you get to experience flying. Usually, the flight is a short one over the front of your handlebars and onto your helmet or upper back. It looks spectacular. All mountain bikers experience such flights eventually. Such an experience usually doesn't result in permanent damage if you have the proper safety equipment. A few moments on your back, mentally checking through all your body parts to make sure you're still in one piece, is a good idea before you try to pop back up. Perhaps a little first aid to stop some bleeding, a quick check to make sure your bike isn't damaged, and you're ready to go, hopefully a bit wiser.

Unhealthy Dwelling

The life principle here is that it's often easier to focus on the negative. When we look in the mirror, our focus is inevitably drawn to our weaknesses and shortcomings. We seem to obsess that we're too much of one thing or not enough of something else. We're too tall or short, our weight isn't right, we don't like our hair, and so on. Our blemishes may be all we see. Our clothes are not in style, or our body is not proportioned as we'd like. Our job isn't right, or those we care about don't respond as we think they should. There are endless ways we tear ourselves down. Just as in mountain biking, if we dwell on these negative aspects, that is what we'll become.

What do I mean? C. S. Lewis put it rather succinctly in the tenth of his fictional *Screwtape Letters* written from a senior devil to his apprentice nephew on how to handle their human subjects. He stated, "All mortals tend to turn into the thing they are pretending to be."[1] Simply, it is that we become comfortable with this kind of negative conversation, and others notice that we seem to be constantly unpleasant, tearing ourselves or others down or just dwelling on ourselves and

1. C. S. Lewis, *The Screwtape Letters* (HarperCollins, 2001), 50.

CHAPTER 1: DWELLING ON OBSTACLES

creating a victim myth in our minds. Left unchecked, this can develop into an ever-accelerating downward spiral of self-esteem.

Unfortunately, those who begin to dwell on the negative do not stop with themselves; they frequently turn to tearing down others, often to protect their fragile self-image. I have known some who have fallen into this pattern and cannot seem to carry on a conversation without including in it someone else's embarrassing failure or weakness. No one really wants to be around such negative conversations. It pushes others away and then of course adds to the individual's downward, self-indulgent spiral. One serious trap associated with this self-victimization is to produce an atmosphere of helplessness in which no responsibility is taken. Everything becomes someone else's fault or is caused by circumstances or unfairness. What we're really telling ourselves is that it's out of our control. The subject of each conversation becomes lost in the trapped individual's growing obsession to prove there's nothing wrong with them and that it's not their fault. (This is discussed at length later in chapter 7.)

One of the telltale indicators of such dwelling is often a change in vocal tone. I call it the Eeyore voice. (I apologize for making you hear this in your head as you read.) You know the voice as Eeyore tells Christopher Robin, "I've lost my tail and I'll never find it again." Breaking out often requires us to dive into the Tigger voice, which promotes positivity. I'm sure you can also hear in your mind Tigger's voice. "The wonderful thing about Tiggers is Tiggers are wonderful things! Their tops are made out of rubber; their bottoms are made out of springs!" I bet you're smiling already! Never forget Tigger's greatest secret—he knows that he's unique. "The most wonderful thing about Tiggers is I'm the only one."[2]

He is just like each of you. You are also wonderful and one-of-a-kind. That means you are precious to your Heavenly Father.

Those caught in this self-defeating trap continue reinforcing the same behavior expecting things to change. They're unable to appreciate that they have the power to change their behavior and produce a different outcome. I remember counseling a young man on this

---

2. "The Wonderful Thing About Tiggers," Fandom, accessed Nov. 11, 2024, https://pooh.fandom.com/wiki/The_Wonderful_Thing_About_Tiggers.

subject a few years ago. I explained to him that he was like a person sitting in a car with a blown transmission. Things weren't working out when he pushed the gas, so his solution was to push even harder on the gas and refuse any help from the mechanic. The result was that he wasted gas and got nowhere. Pursuing the same detrimental behavior more aggressively only uses up more energy without producing a positive result. Unfortunately, this course leads to frustration, anger, and bitterness, which in turn leads to hate and finally personal destruction (as described more completely in chapter 6). This is a wide and well-worn path. Taking responsibility for your own acts or your role in a particular outcome, regardless of how embarrassing or stressful it might be, is empowering. This is a basic step in both repentance and overcoming.

The Better Focus

There is another way. The Apostle Paul counseled the Corinthians about seeing through a glass darkly (see 1 Corinthians 13:9–12). We learn from his letter that we must see ourselves as God sees us and put away childish things. He tells us that drawing closer to the Savior and seeking to see life as it really is, using revelation and truth, will allow us to grow from seeing in part to seeing perfectly. One day, we will see God face-to-face and know ourselves as He knows us. Paul further tells us that we may proceed from glory to glory, thus gaining ever-greater insight and understanding until we see as we are seen and receive a fulness of God's glory in His kingdom (see 2 Corinthians 3:18). Through Joseph Smith, the Lord has stated that this would occur when we stand with Him, having received a fulness of His glory in the celestial kingdom (see Doctrine and Covenants 76:94, 96).

Pursuing this path then allows us to stand in front of that same mirror and learn to see ourselves as God sees us. He sees beyond our frailties and weaknesses, and we can too. When the Lord told Samuel the prophet to go to the house of Jesse, because He had prepared the next king of Israel from among Jesse's sons, Samuel obeyed. Jesse called each son before Samuel. The great prophet initially assumed that the next king was to be the eldest son, Eliab, because he looked the part. The Lord's answer was instructive for Samuel as well as us.

CHAPTER 1: DWELLING ON OBSTACLES

In explaining that it was to be the youngest son, David, the Lord said, "Look not on his countenance, or on the height of his stature . . . for the Lord seeth not as man seeth; for man looketh on the outward appearance, but the Lord looketh on the heart" (1 Samuel 16:7). David was brought in from the fields, and though he didn't look the part, Samuel knew he was to be the next king and anointed him, "and the spirit of the Lord came upon David from that day forward" (1 Samuel 16:13).

We are God's children, loved beyond measure. He is always there for us and has created this existence to allow us to become like Him and return to His presence. It's a process that requires striving, desire, and sincerity rather than perfection. By practicing this, we begin to understand what He sees when He looks at us, and we can dwell on the positive of who we are rather than who we've been. We also then break out of the natural man's tendency to dwell on the past and are able to focus on becoming something more.

There's another interesting side-effect of this kind of thinking. As we think of ourselves differently, we also begin to see others differently. We begin to see others as God sees them, which allows us to more easily feel charity or the pure love of Christ, which, not by accident, is also spoken of in the same chapter of Corinthians as being "the greatest of these" (1 Corinthians 13:13).

You can't avoid the obstacles you're dwelling on. They become part of you. Dwell on things that, as they become part of you, will lift you up, empower you, and make you a better person. It will draw others to you as they sense that spirit of charity you carry. Make yourself the kind of person such that anyone who crosses your path during the day will be grateful for having done so.

2

Focusing Ahead

To access the Mueller Park Trail, you must cross a bridge from the parking lot. There are six more bridges between this spot and Big Rock. The bridge has several two-by-six boards running the length of it for strength and a six-inch drop-off at the end. Staying on the boards and executing a little hop at the end is helpful in avoiding your first little surprise of the trip. This skill comes into play later as you attempt to avoid obstacles and stay on the narrow track or one of the narrow bridges. The trick to riding in a relatively narrow straight line is not to look down at the line itself or even at the front of your tire. I don't know the physics or physiology of it, but bringing your focus too close to the front of your tire dramatically affects your balance. I believe it diminishes your brain's perspective of the environment and therefore results in an inability to balance and maintain a straight course.

Experience has taught me on many different trails that what works best is keeping the center of my focus about fifteen to twenty feet beyond my front tire and using my peripheral vision to pick up the closer-in details as well as the farther-out details. Of course, a biker never stares at one spot—they're always shifting their field of vision, looking around quickly, and maintaining awareness. But the center of that range of movement and view always comes back to the location mentioned.

Focus and Perspective

This focus allows you to anticipate and correct. It allows you to avoid problems and adjust gears as necessary. It creates perspective and balance. All these benefits mean that you can maintain momentum without unnecessary mishaps.

In life, focusing ahead allows you many of the same advantages. We humans tend to act without considering the consequences, or if we recognize the possibility of a negative result, we're quick to discount it as being unlikely to happen to us. This short-term view of life is often referred to as a desire for immediate gratification or simply being shortsighted. This is a view that opens us up to the influence of Satan. It's not the big compromises we make in life that usually steer us away from our eternal goals; it is a series of small deviations that pull us ever farther off course. Virtually all selfish activity, bitterness, hate, indulgence, immorality, self-indulgence, rationalization of things that we know in our hearts are wrong, and other acts that pollute our spirits, our bodies, and our lives consist of a series of small errors or justifications. When taken by themselves, they may seem benign. However, when seen as a connected process, it's clear where they lead.

In *The Screwtape Letters*, the senior and more experienced devil, Screwtape, gives counsel to his young nephew, an apprentice devil named Wormwood, on how to effectively do his job with his specific human "patient." He says in one of his letters, "You will say that these are very small sins; and doubtless, like all young tempters, you are anxious to be able to report spectacular wickedness. But do remember . . . it does not matter how small the sins are provided that their cumulative effect is to edge the man away from the Light and out into the Nothing. . . . Indeed, the safest road to Hell is the gradual one—the gentle slope, soft underfoot, without sudden turnings, without milestones, without signposts."[3]

This illustrates a second important principle: Anyone who begins to fall under the influence of the adversary or his minions will

---

3. C. S. Lewis, *The Screwtape Letters* (HarperCollins, 2001), 60–61.

gradually be robbed of the joy and satisfaction of accomplishing anything worthwhile. They will have access to enjoyment of all the good and uplifting aspects of their life steadily drained away and replaced by "nothing." Examples include the loss of warm relations with friends and family who love and care for them, good health, a desire to serve and grow, involvement in religious devotion, interest in a spiritually and physically healthy lifestyle, enjoyment of wholesome and uplifting activities, and the satisfaction and positive reinforcement that comes with achievement (from good grades, positive reviews at work, or involvement in something that took much effort and has had a very positive result).

The adversary also robs them of the rest that comes with a clear conscience and a life free from the constant and ever-increasing burden of guilt, shame, addiction, or obsession. People often lose motivation to strive, to achieve, and to do their best and even the ability to care.

There can also be a growing tendency to objectify others, treating them as objects that have no right to feel, express opinions, share thoughts, or experience negative impacts from offensive behavior. In short, people around the afflicted individual are not seen as people with rights, needs, or a voice. Screwtape states in the same letter, "He [the human] must not be allowed to suspect that he is now, however slowly, heading right away from the sun on a line which will carry him into the cold and dark of utmost space."[4]

The adversary does not need to get us to take one huge fatal step. He accomplishes the same with distraction from that which is good, leading to a lessening of our interest in positive pursuits and then taking from us all the things that are "something" in our lives and replacing them with "nothing."

"Nothing" doesn't mean empty or a complete void. Such emptiness will always be filled with something. This "nothing" includes those things that serve no positive or productive purpose—behavior that drags us down, like obsessions with computer gaming, music, or various other media that can isolate us from others, addicting substances or behaviors, or obsessions with "things" instead of loved ones.

---

4. Lewis, *Screwtape Letters*, 57.

Satan's Isolation Tactics

This is particularly insidious when it comes to the damage done by the adversary to our spirituality. People with such burdens too often cut themselves off from the community of their ward or family under the counterfeit idea that organized religion is somehow corrupt or hurtful. This most often comes from a difficult experience with one member that is then generalized to the entire ward or Church. Satan then replaces this with a cobbled-together, obscure "spirituality" that consists of picking and choosing traits and practices as if the gospel is a Las Vegas buffet. So those afflicted choose what fits into their chosen lifestyle and reject that which is inconvenient or uncomfortable. The result is a feel-good mishmash that may work when the sun is shining but will be dashed to pieces when storms occur in our lives. Satan always sets us up to fail and desires that when we fail, we take as many people with us as possible. The scriptures are replete with stupendous examples of Satan refusing to support his followers at the last day (see Alma 30:60).

Such things do no more than pointlessly fill time or provide selfish gratification. "Nothing" can also include the replacement of our positive human associations with counterfeit friendships with those who use us to justify their own insecurities or acts. As alluded to in another of Screwtape's letters, the goal is to give us "an ever-increasing craving for an ever-diminishing pleasure."[5] (See also Alma 44.) Why do so many slide into such an abyss? Satan knows that once he has taken from us "everything" we once valued and cherished—that lifted us up and made us feel joy—and replaced it with "nothing," we will accept "anything" he offers because it is "something."

This also works the other way. It is the small, good things we do—the slight corrections as we focus ahead—that make all the difference. The scriptures are replete with examples and counsel encouraging us to appreciate the power of small, positive acts. (We will discuss this at more length in the next chapter.)

As we focus ahead and keep life in perspective, we are then able to more easily recognize, anticipate, and avoid the difficulties that cause

---

5. Lewis, *Screwtape Letters*, 43.

problems along the trail. Our life continues to be something of value, and we consistently build upon the positive choices and acts that bring strength, purpose, and happiness. Now *that* is a trail that leads us somewhere worth going. There's nothing worse than spending large amounts of time getting to a place that, when you arrive, you discover wasn't worth the effort. On the other hand, there's nothing more satisfying than working to achieve new heights of worthwhile spiritual, physical, emotional, or mental accomplishment and discovering the view from the mountain peak upon which you have arrived. That's worth every step along the way.

3
Preparation and Anticipation

PREPARATION

There are certain precautions that should be taken before and while riding that can make the experience much more enjoyable. They can in some cases also help the rider avoid danger, inconvenience, and, on occasion, tragedy. These include the wearing of a proper helmet, gloves, and safety glasses while both ascending and descending. It's not uncommon to see riders going uphill with their helmets unclipped, tied to their backpacks, or even absent. My helmet is not utilized to save my life every time I ride, but there are those times when I have avoided serious injury because I wore it. At the beginning of any ride, I have no idea if today will be one of those days when I was glad I wore my helmet or glasses. Proper gloves make a lot of difference with grip and fatigue, especially on the downhill run.

There's a spot on the trail just before arriving at the "pipeline," which is about halfway to Big Rock, that I took a pretty good spill. It is a steeper rock field of about 100–200 feet. I got out of my anticipated line, and because momentum is limited going uphill, when my front tire fell into a cradle with a solid rock, it stuck perfectly. My body of course continued, without the bike, over the handlebars and onto my helmet and back. I sustained a cut on my leg and a couple of spectacular bruises from landing on the protruding rocks, but there was no permanent damage. How different the story might have been had I left my helmet at home or clipped it to my backpack!

It's also common in the spring or fall to have branches hanging out on the trail. They may catch in your spokes, hit you in the glasses or helmet, or otherwise hinder you. It's not always possible to see them coming. It's also important to remember that your helmet extends your height several inches, so your usual perception of where the top of your head is will not be accurate. During one downward ride, about a half mile from the trailhead, my helmet struck a broken limb that was solid and did not give. It dazed me, and though I remained on my bike, I covered about twenty feet before I regained my senses. I have often wondered what might have happened without my helmet.

Perhaps the worst potential crash I've had came during a road ride. I had covered a long loop and was on the Legacy Trail in Davis County. The last few miles involve negotiating double gates that require the bike rider to weave between some metal barriers prior to crossing the road. I was riding a little faster than I should have, and while attempting to weave, I clipped the front of the second gate. It acted like a pinball bumper and gave just enough to flip me into the back side of the gate I had just negotiated. The second gate flipped me back again, and as my momentum continued forward on the bike, it flipped me backward. My feet were in baskets on the pedals, so as I fell backward, the bike wrenched my feet out, badly spraining my ankle. The worst part of the accident was that I went straight backward onto my head. Fortunately, I had my helmet securely attached, and while I smashed the back of my helmet, my skull remained intact. I have little doubt that if I had not been wearing my helmet, I would have been critically injured or worse. As it was, I lay there for about five minutes groaning in pain and had to ride the remainder of the way home using one ankle. There was a family in a field about twenty yards from this quite spectacular crash that never acknowledged even being aware of my situation.

Proper safety equipment can mean the difference between a brief interruption in your ride and a permanent interruption or change in

CHAPTER 3: PREPARATION AND ANTICIPATION

your life. It's not worth the risk because you may be hot or inconvenienced or think, "That's just the way I am."

The other preparation principle is embodied in the motto I use with my riding buddies: "You condition for the ride up, but you dress for the ride down." The first part of this is obvious—the ride will always be more enjoyable if you're in shape. The second part of the motto is unique to riding in the high mountains. One of the big mistakes made by mountain bikers is that they dress too lightly. This is usually not a factor when riding uphill because of the heat your body generates, particularly in your legs. However, when coming down, you're already wet with sweat, and on a cooler afternoon, it can become quite cold, particularly on the shaded parts of the trail. The wisdom is in making sure you layer so you have something extra to wear on the way down. In the early spring and late fall, this is an even bigger factor since wind chill temperatures going down can differ dramatically. This means that carrying long-fingered and often insulated gloves at certain times of the year is a must. I have several pairs of gloves ranging from padded no-finger gloves for hot days to ski gloves for those rides I take when it's thirty-something degrees in the winter.

The other factor is the weather, which in the mountains can change with little notice. I remember one ride with one of my most frequent riding buddies, Jeff, in mid-June. We got about twenty-five minutes into our ride and were in the last mile before arriving at Big Rock. The temperature was about fifty degrees, and the day was mostly clear and calm. Then, without warning, dark clouds appeared from the northwest directly over the mountain ridge, and within ten minutes, the temperature had dropped to near freezing and we were in a snow blizzard with gusts of wind up to forty miles per hour.

As the wind picked up and the dark clouds streamed over the ridge, we immediately turned around, and before we had traveled a hundred yards downhill, snow was accumulating on the trail. Trees were being blown down, which we had to climb over carrying our bikes on our shoulders, and the metal and plastic brakes on our bikes became ice-cold, making a firm grip increasingly difficult. I happened to have long-fingered gloves, which helped, but Jeff didn't, and with about a half mile to go, his hands were in such bad shape that he could no longer grip his brakes or handlebars. We dismounted and took a shortcut through undergrowth straight down the side of the mountain to what we knew was a picnic area that ran along the bottom of the canyon next to the stream. After jumping a six-foot chain-link fence carrying our bikes and crossing a bridge (which was obstructed by a pine tree with a diameter of at least two feet, which had been blown down and partially destroyed the bridge), we were able to reach the parking lot and find warmth in one of the cars. It was a close one. While hypothermia was stalking us, frostbite and further tragedy were avoided because we turned around immediately and had mostly layered for the cooler ride down.

ANTICIPATION

I will use the term *anticipation* to describe advance adjustment to changing terrain while riding. The principle means recognizing a change in slope, let's say a climb, and making the speed and gear adjustments before you hit the upward grade. This allows momentum and a smooth gear transition to already be in place before they're needed. Maintaining momentum makes the climb easier, while the early gear shift also allows you to avoid the gears shifting under stress during the climb, which can cause the chain to jump or slip while on the hill. A chain that jumps, breaks, comes off, or shifts while you're exerting maximum stress on a climb can cause unexpected slippage, often resulting in a crash or injury. Early shifting before the pressure mounts allows the chain to adjust smoothly without any jerks or slippage.

In addition, anticipating changing conditions ahead can also prevent unnecessary difficulty or accidents. During one winter ride along the Legacy Trail, it seemed relatively dry. However, recent snow melt had resulted in water completely covering the floor of a pedestrian tunnel that runs under one of the highways intersecting the trail. There's no drain for the water in that particular underpass, and it was just cold enough for the water to have uniformly frozen into a perfect ice-skating rink. I noticed the difference in coloration but not its significance. Two-thirds of the way through the tunnel, both tires shot to my right on the ice, causing my bike and me to do a kind of crash and slide to the other side of the tunnel. Sometimes we learn in spite

CHAPTER 3: PREPARATION AND ANTICIPATION

of our own ignorance, and if we survive the experience, we become wiser. In this case, there were no serious injuries, but on wet days, I now approach the underpasses with greater respect.

My final example occurred on my first trip to Moab. We rode several wonderful trails—including Jurassic, Easy, Lazy (which are neither easy nor lazy), and the Dead Horse Point Rim—then returned to our bed and breakfast. Leah wisely decided to rest before dinner, but I wanted to try the famous Slick Rock Trail. I didn't have time to do the long version, so I rode the shorter (but not easier) two-mile loop. I finished all right and had plenty of water with me during the day. However, I learned that the dry heat not only requires ample amounts of water, but it also dries out your body from the outside in. I was hydrated and dehydrated at the same time. I struggled to get to the truck and made it to the B&B but could barely function. I downed a couple of bottles of electrolytes, sat in the hot tub, and rehydrated my entire body from the outside in before I felt normal again. It took about an hour and taught me there is a lot more to surviving dry heat than just drinking liquids.

These principles applied to life are much the same. When we are in difficulty, under stress, or amidst changing conditions, it's too late to prepare or effectively adjust. While it may be possible for some, it's at best much more difficult. We then are forced to endure with what we've got and hope it's enough. Sometimes others are involved who have wisely prepared both for themselves and for us. They may be able to ease the burden, but that's not always the case. Living with the expectation that someone else will always be there to bail you out is naive at best.

PROPER FENCING

Early in World War II, the people of Narvik, Norway, learned this principle the hard way. In the far reaches of northern Norway, Narvik would seem to have been of little interest to the warring powers. However, it was home to a deep seaport that was nearest to large deposits of iron ore, which was highly sought after by the Nazi regime for wartime production. Thus, it was an early target for expansion. After a sharp but brief campaign, the Allies were expelled from

Norway and the Norwegian Army disbanded, leaving its citizens at the mercy of the Third Reich. The sentiments expressed by the mayor of Narvik, Theodor Broch, provide profound insight as he recalled, "It was a harsh land we had . . . but never had it been so delightful, so desirable as now. Our leading men had already been driven abroad. Our ships had sunk or sailed away. All along the border [with Sweden] were young men like myself, thousands more would follow. We had to leave to learn the one craft we had neglected. We had built good homes in the mountains, but we had neglected to fence them properly."[6]

Too often we convince ourselves that we have done enough, that our families are secure, and that our children are safe from the terrible influences that we see devastating other families and society. We grow complacent and neglect the regular protective behavior that is so critical to our family's spiritual well-being. It is during such careless moments when we may have discarded, misplaced, or simply not kept in proper condition the protective armor given to us by God (see Ephesians 6:10–18)—much like the unused helmet clipped to our backpack. Suddenly, circumstance, tragedy, or Satan himself moves against us and we are faced with the trial of our lives. Our excuses that spiritual preparation was inconvenient or demanding—or that we instead chose our own brand of comfortable, cobbled spirituality—then ring hollow.

What then are the steps we must take to prepare properly and anticipate needs in advance of life's trials? First, we must develop a pattern of acting in advance of the need and not allowing circumstances to catch up with us and dictate our actions. This allows us to maintain meaningful freedom of later choice. By not taking advantage of moments when we have the time to choose from a wide array of alternatives and waiting until our options are down to one or two, we allow circumstances or others to dictate to us. Doors of opportunity may have closed, which can leave us in crisis mode. Delaying or abdicating a decision is also a choice. This particular kind of choice can severely limit our freedom to act (see 1 Nephi 14:1–4).

---

6. Martin Gilbert, *The Second World War: A Complete History* (Henry Holt & Company, 1991), 92.

Deepness of the Earth and Good Ground

The secret to real preparation for spiritual challenges is found in one of the Savior's best-known parables. It is repeated in three of the four Gospels, although I will refer here to the Gospel of Mark. It provides insight into the four states of man on this earth with respect to receiving the word of God. It also provides a key understanding of what can constitute the difference between success and failure in spiritual growth.

Mark first tells us that some seeds fell by the wayside but were devoured by involvement with sin and direct control of the adversary (see Mark 4:4, 14–15). Some will make choices that place them on his turf where meaningful freedom to act does not exist.

Another group of seeds fell among thorns and began to grow but were choked by distraction and absorption with the cares of the world (see Mark 4:7, 18–19). These individuals chose to abdicate their freedom to choose.

A further group of seeds fell on stony ground and were unable to gain sufficient root, so when the sun came (the trials of the world), they were scorched, withered, and died (see Mark 4:5–6, 16–17). Their intent was good, and they were perhaps even honest and forthright people, but they failed to prepare adequately, so they were not strong enough to overcome. The first positive clue in how to do it right is given here when the writer tells us that the roots had "no depth of earth" (Mark 4:5).

The last group of seeds fell on good ground and were nourished and grew (see Mark 4:8, 20).

It seems clear that the Savior's parable encourages us to cultivate "good ground," or what is also called "deepness of earth," to enable us to develop deep roots. This allows us to withstand and overcome the difficult times that come as part of life on this earth. How then do we develop this deepness of earth that allows us to be properly prepared and anticipate such times?

In the Sermon on the Mount, the Savior counsels us that as we "hunger and thirst after righteousness" (Matthew 5:6), we will be filled. This regular nourishment that results from our efforts will, if applied with great care, get root and bring forth the fruit of everlasting life (see Alma 32:37, 41). He also warns us in that where there is no nourishment and care, there cannot be fruit (see Matthew 7:16–20). He further advises that we must be patient and diligent and have our eyes looking forward to the successful result, so that we may become "the children of [our] Father which is in heaven" (Matthew 5:45; see also Alma 32:38, 40).

Nourishment doesn't happen all at once. You can't pour the water needed for an entire growing season on the seeds the first day. And you can't expect the seed to grow if the ground is not prepared, tilled, and nourished. Nourishing takes time and occurs little by little. It must be consistently applied over long periods of our lives. We have been given daily, weekly, and monthly resources that we must take advantage of to provide the regular requirement of spiritual nutrients necessary to develop "deepness of earth."

As we develop habits of regular personal and family prayer, personal and family scripture study, family home evening, observance of family meals together, regular church and temple attendance, morality, honesty, service, and development of a heart that is willing to follow the Lord's inspiration wherever it leads, we prepare ourselves for the great trials that are necessary to allow us to become something more. We also obtain the Spirit as our guide so that when we approach difficulties, we can adjust our gears, maintain momentum, and come through the storms we face. We are not promised that this process will leave us unbruised, but we will also not wither and die. We will remain faithfully and deeply rooted in good ground. It is not usually the great one-time sacrifices that help us become who we must be to return to our Heavenly Father; rather, it is the consistent and faithful application of small things that make the difference. The scriptures are replete with such examples and counsel, for God knows we must learn this important principle.

Small Things Are the Big Things

James reminds us, "Behold, we put bits in the horses' mouths, that they may obey us; and we turn about their whole body. Behold also the ships, which though they be so great, and are driven of fierce

CHAPTER 3: PREPARATION AND ANTICIPATION

winds, yet are they turned about with a very small helm, whithersoever the governor listeth" (James 3:3–4).

The Savior taught of the power of even a small amount of faith: "For verily I say unto you, If ye have faith as a grain of mustard seed, ye shall say unto this mountain, Remove hence to yonder place; and it shall remove; and nothing shall be impossible unto you" (Matthew 17:20).

Goliath was defeated and Israel was saved by a small, smooth stone slung by a lad (see 1 Samuel 17:40).

When Naaman came to Elisha to be healed of leprosy, he was given what seemed to be a simple task to be healed. Naaman was reluctant, thinking the task was beneath the captain of the host of the king of Syria, but he was convinced by the argument of his servants to proceed and was healed: "And his servants came near, and spake unto him, and said . . . if the prophet had bid thee do some great thing, wouldest thou not have done it? how much rather then, when he saith to thee, Wash, and be clean? Then went he down, and dipped himself seven times in Jordan, according to the saying of the man of God: and his flesh came again like unto the flesh of a little child, and he was clean" (2 Kings 5:13–14).

The children of Israel were healed by the simple act of obeying the Lord and looking to the brazen serpent that Moses was commanded to raise up (see Numbers 21:4–9).

After fishing through the night and catching nothing, Simon-Peter and his companions were commanded to make a small change in their approach by casting their nets over the right side of the boat. This small act of obedience produced a miraculous result: "Then Jesus saith unto them, Children, have ye any meat? They answered him, No. And he said unto them, Cast the net on the right side of the ship, and ye shall find. They cast therefore, and now they were not able to draw it for the multitude of fishes" (John 21:5–6).

Yes, we know these stories and teachings, but do we really believe as David when he told Goliath, "This day will the Lord deliver thee into mine hand . . . that all the earth may know that there is a God in Israel" (1 Samuel 17:46)? God sent us here to achieve greatness, but great results are accomplished by consistently doing small things.

"Wherefore, be not weary in well-doing, for ye are laying the foundation of a great work. And out of small things proceedeth that which is great. Behold, the Lord requireth the heart and a willing mind" (Doctrine and Covenants 64:33–34).

"Let no man count them as small things; for there is much which lieth in futurity, . . . which depends upon these things. . . . Therefore . . . let us cheerfully do all things that lie in our power" (Doctrine and Covenants 123:15–17).

"Now ye may suppose that this is foolishness in me; but behold I say unto you, that by small and simple things are great things brought to pass . . . and by very small means the Lord doth confound the wise and bringeth about the salvation of many souls" (Alma 37:6–7).

God did not send us here to be in some mysterious "escape room" for His pleasure and entertainment. He gave us all the answers, guidance, and instructions necessary to overcome every challenge we would face. In fact, he laid out the entire process of developing faith and turning it into knowledge in Alma 32 just in case we can't connect the dots ourselves. The poor and destitute of the Zoramites asked a simple question: "What shall we do?" (Alma 32:9). The entire chapter is essentially a step-by-step guided answer to that question, ending with, "Then, my brethren, ye shall reap the rewards of your faith, and your diligence, and patience, and long-suffering, waiting for the tree to bring forth fruit unto you" (Alma 32:43).

He also knows we cannot do this work alone. This is the specific reason He has created an organization where we can help each other in an organized way under the direction of prophetic guidance, make and keep sacred covenants, and receive the ordinances and gifts He has prepared to guide us through the confusion and tumult He knew we would face. We are truly never alone unless we intentionally make ourselves so.

Know that there is a God in the world today and that nothing is impossible for Him. It takes faith and inspiration to prepare for winter on a sunny day. It takes deep roots in good ground during winter storms to know that spring will return. It takes time every day to build and organize a righteous life and family. Every small moment is worth it.

4

Riding with a Guide and Knowing the Trail

THE MUELLER PARK TRAIL CAN BE DAUNTING THE FIRST TIME. THE first hundred-yard stretch includes a couple of rather steep uphill climbs, which can completely drain the uninitiated. The first mile of the trail is also generally much steeper than the following 2.5 miles to Big Rock. There are also many blind corners that can be just as hazardous when traffic is light as they are on more congested days. As a result, it's a very good idea to invite someone on your first trip who has experience on that trail.

An experienced guide has knowledge and perspective. They know when more demanding parts of the trail will be confronted and when it'll ease up. I've seen individuals in otherwise excellent condition collapse in seizures of nausea on their first attempt by overextending themselves during the first mile of the trail. A guide who knows the trail can help keep the difficult parts in perspective, thus preventing those who depend on their wisdom from becoming exhausted, discouraged, or losing hope. A thoughtful guide will direct you when to rest, ensure the group has sufficient water, and know how to tackle the trail to minimize wasted energy. They will also encourage those who follow and uplift them during difficult moments by giving them hope that they are progressing toward their goal.

Travel in the mountains should always be approached with respect. Weather conditions can change rapidly. The trail itself can change dramatically in its technical aspects depending on the time of year, recent weather, or current weather. A switchback turn is different in the fall—with wet, slippery leaves on the ground or when muddy after a good rain—than it is during the dry part of the summer. Wet or muddy brakes perform differently than dry ones. The temperature can also provide challenges. It's possible to experience everything from hypothermia to heat exhaustion on the same trail depending on the circumstances and time of year.

This means that you need to know the trail and how it can change given any set of circumstances. The first time I rode the trail, I wasn't properly conditioned for such a ride. However, my guide, Jonathan, was reasonably well acquainted with the trail and knew where a novice might need to stop to catch their breath along the way. He helped me pace myself and remain hydrated. The result was love at first ride. I immediately realized that this ride offered a great workout, without being a man-killer, as long as you were in shape and properly prepared. As I became more familiar with the trail and started introducing others to it, I followed the example of my original guide. I recall introducing my son Howie to the trail when he was quite young. He has always been in great shape, but he didn't have a mountain bike at the time and had only a few gears. I was amazed at how much just a little encouragement and a few well-timed breaks did to make the experience enjoyable for him. Now, of course, he would need to back way off the pedals for me to keep up!

One of the most dangerous aspects of the trail is restricted visibility due to the frequency of blind corners and overgrown foliage. This makes the trail different from almost any other I've ridden. Anyone using this trail must be constantly aware to avoid collisions or accidents caused by changing aspects of the trail itself. This is especially true of those using it for mountain biking. A good guide will know when they're approaching a sight-restricted section and slow down, and a really good guide will call out and provide that information to anyone who may be out of sight. It does no good to know the trail if

CHAPTER 4: RIDING WITH A GUIDE AND KNOWING THE TRAIL

you don't do anything with the knowledge. A rider who knows the trail well but disregards that knowledge and showboats, or continues at speeds that will not allow them to avoid an accident, is simply foolish and a hazard to themself and others. That kind of rider should never be a guide.

THINKING ERRORS: WE DON'T NEED GOD'S HELP

It's a great blessing during this life to have many along the way who can guide us on proper paths and help us anticipate hazards, slow down, rest, or work harder at the appropriate times. Such guides can strengthen our knees when feeble or lift us up with hope when our hands hang down (see Isaiah 35:3–4; Doctrine and Covenants 81:4–5). Our Heavenly Father provides many who are available to help in times of distress or to warn us of danger or disaster ahead. We can only benefit if we heed their advice and if we use our own talents, experience, and knowledge wisely. Such an important principle deserves one more example.

I have enjoyed scuba diving for over forty years. During the 1980s, I had the opportunity to do quite a bit of diving in the Cayman Islands. What a beautiful location for any activity but especially diving. The water is clear, most of the dives involve little or no current due to the reef surrounding most of the island, and the sea life is plentiful, diverse, and colorful. On one occasion, I chose to go night diving with a friend. We joined about a dozen others, and the guide boat took us about a half mile offshore but still within the reef. At night there are many different creatures out: octopuses, lobster, and the occasional free-swimming moray or spotted eel. It's also interesting to see the parrotfish that blow bubbles around their bodies and appear to sleep vertically in the water. Your vision of the surroundings is restricted to the beam of your flashlight, and when you turn your flashlight off, you'll find that it's pitch black. At night, navigation is even more important, even though the dive boat will leave a bright light hanging underwater as a beacon to aid in your return to the boat. On this occasion, my friend and I swam about a hundred yards from the boat.

Clear water is not really clear, with sediment and sea life suspended in the water and with the pitch black of night; at about thirty yards, it's not possible to see the underwater light from the boat. We were careful to note the underwater formations so we would be able to find our way back by bottom navigation.

We were in about thirty feet of water and were unsure which way to return, so we surfaced to look for the boat. On my way up, I noticed that my flashlight could illuminate the bottom from about twenty feet above, but the light could not give me a view of the bottom for the last ten feet to the surface. We surfaced and located the direction of the boat, then I told my friend that I would go first and felt that I could keep a straight course for ten feet until I saw the bottom. Bottom navigation would be straightforward from that point. I dove, and the plan was for him to follow. Before I got ten feet under the water, my dive buddy grabbed my fin and gestured that I surface.

After surfacing, he told me that immediately upon beginning my dive, I curved ninety degrees away from the boat and would have headed off in the wrong direction. We determined to swim on the surface until we could see the underwater light hanging from the boat and then dive and follow it to the ladder. I was absolutely certain when I dove into the dark that I could keep my orientation for ten feet. When I did it, I felt I had stayed exactly on course. The truth was that I had not, and we could have ended up far from the boat and lost in the ocean. Fortunately, my dive buddy was a good guide that night and corrected me. We then adjusted our plan and chose wisely to follow the surface lights until we could see the submerged lights and were fine.

The lesson learned was that there are times when we may be absolutely confident in our direction and may not realize how disorienting the situation might be. Good friends, a spouse who is on the right track, or an inspired leader are placed in our lives for a reason. This is no accident, for God understands well that we cannot make it alone and that helping each other is an integral part of His plan of happiness. There are times when our perspective is not sufficient to help us make course corrections. My perspective, in this case, was completely off. Heavenly Father has not placed us on earth alone. There are others at various times during our life that have the perspective we do not, and they can provide gentle direction that, if listened to humbly, will keep us on course despite ourselves.

The Ultimate Perspective

We also have a powerful guide in the Holy Ghost. He can enlighten and teach us of all things, many of which we cannot learn in any other way (see John 14:26; Moroni 10:5; 2 Nephi 32:5). On the trail, there are often unexpected obstacles, rapid changes in circumstances, and surprise encounters, just as there are in life. Our ability to maintain open communication with the Spirit can allow us to avoid many of the difficulties we might otherwise encounter. The Spirit will be our teacher and guide if we listen and are worthy of His presence. If we choose to disregard or rationalize such guidance, we do so at our own peril. Relying only on ourselves can work when there are no surprises, but it sets us up for a fall when there are.

Paul taught that "the natural man receiveth not the things of the Spirit of God: for they are foolishness unto him: neither can he know them, because they are spiritually discerned" (1 Corinthians 2:14). The Lord further revealed in these latter days that "they [who will not hear the word of the Lord] have strayed from mine ordinances, and have broken mine everlasting covenant; They seek not the Lord . . . but every man walketh in his own way and after the image of his own god . . . which shall fall" (Doctrine and Covenants 1:14–16).

The world today seems full of those who have fallen into the trap of "Thanks, God—I can take it from here." Some believe they can pick and choose what works for them, as if in a religious buffet, and disregard anything that makes them feel uncomfortable or is inconvenient given how they want to behave. They ignore guidance and personal revelation, thinking they already know. In fact, the most frequent statement we seem to hear uttered from childhood to adulthood is "I know." In modern usage, it often means, "I don't want to hear anything else from you." This is most often uttered when being reminded of something we've become a bit careless about. My response to our children whenever they utter this phrase is to say, "I'm glad that you know, but I'm interested in seeing if you *do.*" It is *doing* something with what we know that matters. Satan and his followers know, but they do not do. That was the difference between us and them in keeping our first estate (see Jude 1:6; Abraham 3:26). Knowing is meaningless if you don't use your knowledge with wisdom and practice it in action. Saying "I know" often cuts short a moment when we have an opportunity to receive needed guidance from those with experience, such as parents, grandparents, or spiritual leaders. And worse, it can prevent us from seeking guidance through humble prayer. The Spirit certainly cannot teach us through the interference of our own hubris.

THE POP-CULTURE TRAP

Pop culture and convenient beliefs abound and are wholly insufficient; we must develop real conviction regarding God's plan, our own value, and the reality of Jesus's sacrifice. It's critical that we learn what that sacrifice does to give us the strength to overcome the trials we all will certainly face at some point along the trail. James Russell Lowell—poet, diplomat, and Harvard professor—wrote in his contemporary essay on Abraham Lincoln, "The only faith that wears well and holds its color in all weathers is that which is woven of conviction and set with the sharp mordant of experience."[7]

Thomas Paine, an eighteenth-century American patriot, also emphasized the need for something more when he said, speaking to those of his time, "These are the times that try men's souls. The summer soldier and the sunshine patriot will, in this crisis, shrink from the service of their country; but he that stands by it now, deserves the love and thanks of man and woman. Tyranny, like hell, is not easily conquered; yet we have this consolation with us, that the harder the conflict, the more glorious the triumph. What we obtain too cheap, we esteem too lightly."[8]

This combination of consistent application of faith and conviction with experience produces true conversion. A strong witness of the Holy Ghost and well-absorbed experience are critical to those who seek to develop such deep conviction and true conversion (see Romans 8:16; 1 John 5:6; Hebrews 10:15). True conversion may then be described as the natural result of testimony and knowledge put into action consistently and faithfully (see Acts 3:19; Luke 22:32). Thus, the

---

7. James Russell Lowell, "The Only Faith," BrainyQuote, accessed Nov. 11, 2024, https://www.brainyquote.com/quotes/james_russell_lowell_151382.

8. Thomas Paine, "The Crisis [Dec. 23, 1776]," USHistory.org, accessed Nov. 11, 2024, http://www.ushistory.org/Paine/crisis/c-01.htm.

CHAPTER 4: RIDING WITH A GUIDE AND KNOWING THE TRAIL

truly converted individual becomes a new creature (see 2 Corinthians 5:17), capable of remaining steadfast and strengthening people around them. It's so much more than just belief or knowledge.

We see this in recent guidance from living prophets that emphasizes the importance of a full conversion in addition to having a testimony: "The Holy Ghost will help identify the personal changes you need to make for full conversion. The Lord can then bless you more abundantly. Your *faith* in Him will be fortified, your capacity to *repent* will increase, and your power to *consistently obey* will be reinforced."[9] Conversion has been previously described as testimony and knowledge put into action consistently and faithfully. Elder Scott refers to it as "the fruit or the reward for repentance and obedience."[10]

Knowing you need to lift weights, for example, will not make you stronger; you need to do it consistently and faithfully. This is a simple truth. The Holy Ghost can help us prepare for portions of our personal trail that are harder to identify or more challenging than they appear. Those who are "faithful over a few things" when He manifests Himself unto them, and do not harden their hearts, are given a promise that they will be a "ruler over many things" and enter into the "joy of the Lord" (Matthew 25:21). They are also promised that there will be a "taking away of their stumbling blocks . . . and they will be a blessed people . . . forever . . . and shall no more be confounded" (1 Nephi 14:1–2).

Conversely, those who harden their hearts and turn away from God to follow blind guides set up by the devil and his children will discover there is no acceptable substitute. "Not every one that saith unto me, Lord, Lord, shall enter into the kingdom of heaven; but he that doeth the will of my Father which is in heaven. Many will say to me in that day, Lord, Lord, have we not prophesied in thy name? And in thy name have cast out devils? and in thy name done many wonderful works? And then will I profess unto them, I never knew you: depart from me, ye that work iniquity" (Matthew 7:21–23). Those who harden their hearts and fail to hearken to their spiritual and earthly

---

9. Richard G. Scott, "Full Conversion Brings Happiness," *Ensign* or *Liahona*, May 2002, 26; emphasis in original.

10. Richard G. Scott, "Full Conversion Brings Happiness," 25.

guides cannot avoid falling into the very pit they dig for others (see Psalm 9:15; 1 Nephi 14:3).

As we learn to access the Holy Ghost and follow our inspired earthly guides, we will find the trail much easier and avoid unnecessary first aid along the way.

5

Momentum and Practice

THERE'S A PRINCIPLE I LEARNED AS A COMPETITIVE SWIMMER IN HIGH school and college that I relearned on the mountain track years later. It is such a profound lesson that those who have not experienced it may think it sounds unfair, almost like cheating, but of course it's not. The principle is that of momentum. In the swimming pool, you discover that as you master the technical aspects of a particular stroke and improve your speed and conditioning, swimming actually becomes more efficient and easier. In other words, as a swimmer learns to become more hydrodynamic, they get faster and can maintain that speed because of conditioning; their body actually approaches a more efficient plane on the water, which requires less energy. Yes, a fast swimmer uses less energy than a slower one given similar effort.

Many of us have seen novice swimmers struggle with heads-up breathing and leg- and hip-heavy swimming. This creates such a drag that it's nearly impossible to make meaningful headway. By comparison, watching accomplished swimmers in high school, college, or Olympic competitions as they efficiently move through the water is like seeing art in motion. It's not a coincidence that many swimming teams have one particularly fast swimmer nicknamed "fish."

The same is true with trail riding. As the rider's conditioning improves and they become technically solid, they can move up the trail with the same cadence in a lower gear and gain sufficient speed to allow many of the uphill portions of the trail to be negotiated with little additional energy other than a gear shift. I call this "rolling the hill" because it doesn't feel like you're climbing but rather just rolling over rises in the trail. In addition, rocky areas that jar the slower rider can be almost effortlessly skimmed over by the experienced, balanced rider with momentum. This is not to suggest that speed is everything; out-of-control speed certainly is momentum, but that type of momentum puts you in a position of being a hazard.

Controlled Spiritual Momentum

The ability to sustain controlled momentum is a result of conditioning and has to do with the combination of practice and wisdom. A great swimmer who doesn't work out can't sustain their technique regardless of their knowledge. A conditioned mountain biker who ignores changing conditions and obstacles ends up in an accident, the severity of which is dependent on variables out of their control. In both these situations, the individual may boast or rationalize their freedom to choose not to prepare, exercise good judgment, or do enough conditioning. However, in reality, they have dramatically reduced their freedom and ability to influence the outcome and in fact become bound or "acted upon" (see 2 Nephi 2:14, 26). Peter described the situation clearly: "While they promise them liberty, they themselves are the servants of corruption: for of whom a man is overcome, of the same is he brought in bondage" (2 Peter 2:19).

During my sixties, I became involved with a gentleman named Creighton Rider. He had the disease we call Lou Gehrig's disease, or ALS. It's a devastating, progressive disease that slowly robs your muscles and nervous system of voluntary action. I had known him for years, but only after he contracted ALS did we engage in what's called the "Saints to Sinners" bicycle race. It's a 520-mile race from Salt Lake City to Las Vegas held during the hottest part of the summer (the end of July and beginning of August). It runs for two straight days and primarily involves relays of ten bikers per team, although there are smaller teams and even individuals who participate. I've ridden the race three times and for years, Creighton also rode using a double bike with him using his legs in the front seat and his wife Lisa pedaling and steering on the back. I often rode between 150 and 185 miles, often alone (for my parts of the relay) but also sometimes accompanying others on my team for encouragement and support. There were often about a hundred riders in several teams that participated as part of what was called "Creighton's Riders."

I discovered an extraordinary truth the first time I participated. Each leg of the relay averaged about twenty miles, and as the race went on, heat and fatigue became factors. However, there was a point at which I broke through a mental and emotional barrier that I had unknowingly created within myself. Once on the other side of the barrier, I discovered new reserves of energy and ability I had not realized I possessed. Had I not pushed myself through what I thought was the limit, I would never have discovered what lay on the other side.

The requirement then is for us to actively and consistently practice the basic principles we are taught by our guides (see chapter 4). These include sincere prayer and thoughtful study of the ancient and modern word of God. They include seeking to obtain and regularly use a temple recommend and be involved in faithful service to others in addition to simply attending church meetings. Having regular family home evenings and setting aside time for daily family meals are additional ways we strengthen our ability to receive guidance. Family prayer and scripture study also provide significant additional power not available in personal study and prayer alone. These and other areas provide the basic nutrients for proper and wise spiritual growth. These daily and regular requirements condition your spirit and allow access to the Holy Ghost so that you can maintain momentum during times of trial and wisely exercise proper perspective and understanding of God's will.

THE WORLD'S ABSTRACT, NEUTRALIZED SPIRITUALITY

One of the great falsehoods of modern secular society is that pursuing personal ad hoc spirituality is okay, but organized religion is corrupt, false, and a waste of time. The implication is obvious. Selfishness and idolatry are the counterfeit gospel. Practical real-life experience (and the world itself) tells us that none of us can make it alone. We need each other for at least two reasons. First, we may receive insight and support from others to expand our understanding without having to make every single mistake ourselves. This support can also come at critical times when our physical or spiritual reserves seem spent. Second, the opportunity to help and serve others is itself a principle that elevates our lives and brings us closer to Christ through loving others as ourselves (see Mark 12:3). This allows us to break through those perceived barriers and discover the treasures of wisdom and joy that lie on the other side.

How do we identify spiritual momentum? One indicator is the willingness of our heart and mind to seek and follow God's will. Not only is this an indication that a person is prepared for baptism and reiterated in the sacrament prayer (see Mosiah 18:8–9; Doctrine and Covenants 20:37, 77), but it is also repeatedly reinforced as a requirement for endurance during these latter days (see Doctrine and Covenants 64:34). God made this clear to Solomon: "Know thou the God of thy father, and serve him with a perfect heart and with a willing mind: for the Lord searcheth all hearts, and understandeth all the imaginations of the thoughts: if thou seek him, he will be found of thee" (1 Chronicles 28:9). He also made it clear for us through Paul: "Now therefore perform the doing of it; that as there was a readiness to will, so there may be a performance also out of that which ye have. For if there be first a willing mind, it is accepted according to that a man hath" (2 Corinthians 8:11–12).

Sadly, there exist individuals who have served faithfully for decades only to become fatigued and less involved in actively participating in the gospel. Such individuals often justify their lack of involvement as being due to the requirements of the gospel being too great or restrictive or because of some offense that they claim they can never forget or forgive. This frequently turns into rationalization for taking an easier path. Some play down the eternal seriousness of this type of decision by simply saying they have "stepped away" from the Church. Of course, one does not need to have served faithfully to decide to travel the easier road. There are many inviting trailheads to choose from that lead nowhere. A person can fill their life with busy activities

CHAPTER 5: MOMENTUM AND PRACTICE

or isolated inactivity that serve no productive purpose, even though they may not be considered overtly harmful.

Brother Bradley R. Wilcox described this worldly trap well when he said:

> Your covenant relationship with God and Jesus Christ is a relationship of love and trust in which you have access to a greater measure of Their grace—Their divine assistance, endowment of strength, and enabling power. That power is not just wishful thinking, a lucky charm, or self-fulfilling prophecy. It is real. . . . I testify that you are loved—and you are trusted—today, in 20 years, and forever. Don't sell your birthright for a mess of pottage. Don't trade everything for nothing. Don't let the world change you when you were born to change the world.[11]

SATAN'S ROLLER-COASTER TRAP

Several members of my family love roller coasters. I'm the one who typically offers to stand on the firm ground and take pictures. I'm sure you know why—I simply can't deal with all the twists and turns. There are some amazing roller coasters nowadays, but no matter how exotic they look, there's one principle they all have in common. After a brief, exhilarating ride, they all do the same thing: drop you off exactly where you started. That's right—you have gone nowhere.

There's nothing wrong with this, of course—on a roller coaster. But in life, we're offered opportunities for almost countless diversions. These real-life roller coasters may be thrilling for a moment, but they also don't take us anywhere worth being when we get there. They can, however, divert us from progress and meaning and destroy relationships for years. I have known individuals who have spent decades riding every roller coaster that came along, telling themselves that they're "free" or "spontaneous" or simply that they want to experience everything. They end up middle-aged, alone, and often broken—if they survive that long. Satan can and will march an endless buffet of counterfeit, destructive diversions past us. If we jump at the bait, we

---

11. Bradley R. Wilcox, "O Youth of the Noble Birthright," *Liahona*, Nov. 2024.

will get more and more until, in the end, we have nothing of value and life has become one long, meaningless roller coaster to nowhere.

It's only when we strive to fill our lives with the highest and best activities, including service toward others, that our faith is fully expressed and true conversion is evident. In doing so, we build and maintain the necessary spiritual momentum to ultimately become the type of people we must be to be justified before God (see James 2:14–26). In the end, our faith and our actions are less about what we do than who we are becoming. Too many in the world today are on a path to become little or nothing. It is a world of distraction, wasted time, and missed opportunities. President Dallin H. Oaks stated, "Some uses of individual and family time are better, and others are best. We have to forego some good things in order to choose others that are better or best because they develop faith in the Lord Jesus Christ and strengthen our families."[12]

The easier path in the long run—and usually in the shorter run as well—is the Lord's path. Those turning from the marked path find that without the Spirit and the Lord's guidance, the trials of this world are simply too much for a person to surmount on their own (see preface). Further, there comes with this disconnection a loss of ability to clearly make decisions. Why? Because you lose the ability to discern between God's advice, your own rationalization, and the world's direction. Satan is a master at producing such confusion. This is not a new problem; as Isaiah prophesied, "Woe unto them that call evil good, and good evil; that put darkness for light, and light for darkness; that put bitter for sweet, and sweet for bitter!" (Isaiah 5:20).

Practice and mastery of gospel principles and Christlike attitudes require doing and being. Maintaining momentum requires us to practice doing the right things. The right things consist of those correct principles taught from on high through receiving personal divine guidance, seeking diligently to understand the word of God, and hearkening to the counsel of our religious leaders as they're inspired by the Holy Ghost (see John 16:13; 2 Timothy 3:16; 2 Peter 1:18–21). Robert Frost said it beautifully in an excerpt from his poem "The Road Not Taken":

---

12. Dallin H. Oaks, "Good, Better, Best," *Ensign* or *Liahona*, Nov. 2007, 107.

CHAPTER 5: MOMENTUM AND PRACTICE

Two roads diverged in a yellow wood,
And sorry I could not travel both
And be one traveler, long I stood
And looked down one as far as I could
To where it bent in the undergrowth; . . .

I shall be telling this with a sigh
Somewhere ages and ages hence:
Two roads diverged in a wood, and I—
I took the one less traveled by,
And that has made all the difference.[13]

When you choose to enter the strait gate and follow the narrow path, you are choosing the path "less traveled by." It requires vigilance, effort, and practice to negotiate it well. As you hold to the true course, you build spiritual momentum and find the rest God promised to Moses when He said, "My presence shall go with thee, and I will give thee rest" (Exodus 33:14). Such a choice makes all the difference and allows each traveler to break through their own perceived limitations and experience the extraordinary beauty and freedom on the other side.

---

13. Robert Frost, "The Road Not Taken," Poets.org, accessed Nov. 11, 2024, https://poets.org/poem/road-not-taken.

6

Awareness and Utilizing Gifts

FOR MANY YEARS, I LOOKED FORWARD TO PUTTING THE OBSERVA-tions of this chapter on paper because they apply to so many situations. Riding along a narrow single track with drop-offs and limited visibility produces potential difficulties that are rarely encountered on wider trails or paved paths. Even most single-track mountain bike trails have much better visibility than you can find at Mueller Park. This makes the Mueller Park ride beautiful, interesting, and sometimes unexpectedly hazardous. There are dozens of blind spots that exist just in the first 3.5 miles from the bridge at the trailhead to Big Rock. As stated, the trail can be busy, and even when it's not, it seems that just when a rider begins to feel they're alone on the hill, they round a corner and see another person on their way up or down.

This situation requires constant vigilance, knowledge of the trail, and the use of all your senses, especially your sense of hearing. I'll focus on hearing and speech here because these are often ignored by those on the trail and can mean the difference between a pleasant outing and an unpleasant incident.

With the digital age in full bloom, it's not uncommon to see a hiker, jogger, or even biker with headphones or earbuds. While music or an audiobook may make the trip more enjoyable, it puts them at a disadvantage. It can produce a situation that's hazardous for both the user and others. A person with both ears absorbed by such a device has diminished or no auditory capacity. They can't hear a bike approaching from either direction. If they also have their head down, they may have little or no advance warning, even from the front. From the rear, they're unlikely to hear a rider call out to them courteously or as a warning, and in many cases, it's necessary to actually touch them on the shoulder to inform them that you'd like to pass from behind. They certainly have little opportunity to hear another person coming from around the corner. This is difficult on the clear stretches of trail because so many hike, jog, or ride with their heads down as mentioned. And it's much more dangerous when approaching a blind corner. Proper courtesy on the trail is to call out verbally when approaching a blind stretch and let people know you're a biker, runner, or hiker and if you're headed up or down. If you hear such a warning, it's appropriate to respond by communicating back your status, letting them know you're there.

This is easy to do. If two people are going in the same direction, it's easy to let the slower traveler know you're coming well ahead of time so they can step to the side if necessary. These actions are both common sense and courteous. Unfortunately, there are occasionally those on the hill who treat it like a racecourse (read this as "out-of-control momentum for the conditions or limitations of the trail") in both directions, compounding the risk they create for themselves and others by not communicating and occasionally having earbuds in. However, even a person using the trail at responsible speeds can have an accidental meeting if they ignore this advice.

Accidents occur every year, some serious, because of failure to follow these simple, common-sense rules of courtesy and safety. A person can't deaden or disregard their senses and get very far on the trail. Deadening your sense of hearing going up the trail is like driving in the wrong lane on a curvy mountain highway without a rearview mirror—you're a danger to those in both directions. Doing so on the way down, and compounding it by not communicating, is like driving on a dark night with your lights off and your eyes closed. Both situations place your well-being and enjoyment out of your control and into a stranger's hands. You're at the mercy of circumstance in the hope that the stranger will be exercising responsible behavior.

Some bikers have a bell, which is great for avoiding surprising an animal, but humans don't have such sensitive hearing, particularly around corners. Others say nothing even when communication is attempted.

I remember once on my way down, I was approaching a particularly sharp turn with a hundred-foot drop-off just twelve inches to my right. I knew that just around the corner, anyone coming up would be struggling with the last few feet of a pretty steep, rocky climb. I would probably have called out anyway, but I felt a particularly strong impression and called, "Biker coming down! Biker on the corner!" and in the distance, I heard a very tired response: "I'm here." I slowed, and as I rounded the corner, there was another biker struggling to get to a resting spot. He turned to me and simply said, "How did you know I was there?" My response was "I didn't—that's why I called out." He thanked me and we both continued.

An added courtesy is to remember that it's much tougher going up than coming down. Those I ride with will stop and pull their bikes to the side to allow hikers, joggers, or bikers going up to do so without having to disrupt their momentum. If the downhill rider can't stop and pull over to the side so the uphill traveler doesn't have to detour around or stop, it's a sure indication that the downhill rider is not exercising proper control.

The World Would Deaden Your Spirit

There's an obvious parallel in life. The world today is full of those things that would deaden our temporal and spiritual awareness. It is not accidentally so. This deadening has been well described in its most extreme form by some who endured and survived concentration camps during World War II. Viktor Frankl wrote, "First . . . there was his [a new prisoner's] boundless longing for his home and his family . . . then there was disgust . . . with all the ugliness which surrounded him."[14] He continued, "At first the prisoner looked away. . . . He could not bear to see. . . . Days or weeks later things changed. . . .

14. Viktor E. Frankl, *Man's Search For Meaning* (Simon & Schuster, 1984), 33.

The prisoner stood with . . . detachment. . . . He heard a scream and saw . . . a comrade . . . punished . . . but the prisoner . . . did not avert his eyes any more. By then his feelings were blunted, and he watched unmoved."[15] The conclusion was that the prisoner entered a state "of relative apathy, in which he achieved a kind of emotional death."[16]

While the situation Viktor Frankl found himself in was extreme, more subtle forms of this process of emotional deadening and death occur all around us. Elder Richard G. Scott made it quite clear when he said, "I share a warning. Satan is extremely good at blocking spiritual communication by inducing individuals, through temptation, to violate the laws upon which spiritual communication is founded."[17] He further stated, "The inspiring influence of the Holy Spirit can be overcome or masked by strong emotions, such as anger, hate, passion, fear, or pride. . . . Strong emotions overcome the delicate promptings of the Holy Spirit."[18]

I have known those who I have considered shining examples of the gospel of Jesus Christ who become entangled in such emotional deadening. These are individuals who in the early stages would never consider intentionally rebelling against God's word. They were active churchgoers and inspiring examples of service. However, somewhere along the line, they began to carry anger or offense in their hearts over some event. This was allowed to fester because, in this case, they felt they were somehow justified in not exercising Christlike forgiveness. Some of them, by some twisted gymnastics of rationalization, even convinced themselves they were doing it for a righteous purpose or that they had discovered some more "enlightened" way to get closer to God.

Anger and hubris always have their own purpose, and it is never righteousness, regardless of what we tell ourselves. It was tragic to see, over a period of months or years, this anger become bitterness and then the cold millstone of hate. Such emotions not only mask an

---

15. Frankl, *Man's Search For Meaning*, 33–34.

16. Frankl, *Man's Search For Meaning*, 33.

17. Richard G. Scott, "To Acquire Spiritual Guidance," *Ensign* or *Liahona*, Nov. 2009, 8.

18. Richard G. Scott, "To Acquire Spiritual Guidance," 8.

CHAPTER 6: AWARENESS AND UTILIZING GIFTS

ability to receive spiritual guidance, but they slowly push out all other desirable Christlike traits until wicked emotions and selfishness are all that's left. It's heartbreaking to watch someone you care for slip into darkness and flirt with the damnation of their soul.

As Paul said, "Let every soul be subject unto the higher powers. For there is no power but of God: the powers that be are ordained of God. Whosoever therefore resisteth the power, resisteth . . . God: and they that resist shall receive to themselves damnation" (Romans 13:1–2). Nephi referred quite graphically to "awful chains" when he said, "For behold, at that day shall [Satan] rage in the hearts of the children of men, and stir them up to anger against that which is good . . . until he grasps them with his awful chains, from whence there is no deliverance" (2 Nephi 28:20–22). There is no shortage of counsel in the scriptures about the danger of anger, wrath, and rage. Job tells us that wrath has only the power to kill (see Job 5:2), while James reminds us that it cannot produce righteousness (see James 1:20), and Paul states simply, "For God hath not appointed us to wrath, but to obtain salvation by our Lord Jesus Christ" (1 Thessalonians 5:9).

This trap is as difficult to escape as any addiction because it starts quietly and feeds on itself, and its early stages can be masked and justified so easily. In addition, anger must have a focal point. Those engulfed often begin by focusing on the easier targets first—more distant acquaintances. These targets can avoid or slip away, and over time, since anger must have a focus, such individuals begin to target those who remain—ever closer relations.

The entrapped soul gradually pushes away others until all that is left are the very closest relations who love and care and can help the most. Unfortunately, hate and anger are no respecter of relationships, and they continue to require targets. These closest and most loving of relationships are next on the list, and their ability to help is crushed. Their tragic choice is to either lose their identity and become objectified or an enabling sycophant, or else be targeted. Eventually, these once seemingly unbreakable relationships are destroyed. With no one left, Satan has the individual in a position to target themselves, with often tragic results. He is a master at getting those under such influence to dig a pit for their neighbor, which becomes their own prison (see Psalm 9:15; 141:10; Proverbs 28:10; Ecclesiastes 10:8; Doctrine and Covenants 109:25; 1 Nephi 14:3; 22:14).

Anger and hate are a tragic foundation. They do not exist without self-deceit and selfishness. The process that has led countless individuals and civilizations to become separated from God by iniquity, or "ripe in iniquity" (1 Nephi 17:35), and ready for destruction has always involved this at its core. Jesus lamented the wickedness of the people in Jerusalem, saying, "O Jerusalem, Jerusalem, thou that killest the prophets, and stonest them which are sent unto thee, how often would I have gathered thy children together, even as a hen gathereth her chickens under her wings, and ye would not!" (Matthew 23:37).

Jesus went on to prophesy of the destruction of Jerusalem and the sorrows of the last days, including our days, "For nation shall rise against nation, and kingdom against kingdom: and there shall be famines, and pestilences, and earthquakes, in divers places. All these are the beginning of sorrows. . . . And then shall many be offended, and shall betray one another, and shall hate one another. . . . And because iniquity shall abound, the love of many shall wax cold" (Matthew 24:7–12). He closes His prophecy by telling the disciples, "If that evil servant shall say in his heart, My lord delayeth his coming; And shall begin to smite his fellowservants, and to eat and drink with the drunken; The lord of that servant shall come in a day when he looketh not for him. . . . And shall cut him asunder, and appoint him his portion with the hypocrites: there shall be weeping and gnashing of teeth" (Matthew 24:48–51).

One of the best-chronicled examples of this may be found in the final destruction of the Nephite civilization. Mormon's final recorded letter to his son speaks for itself: "I fear lest the Lamanites shall destroy this people; for they do not repent, and Satan stirreth them up continually to anger one with another. Behold, I am laboring with them [the Nephites] continually. . . . I fear lest the Spirit of the Lord hath ceased striving with them. For so exceedingly do they anger that it seemeth me that they have no fear of death; and they have lost their love, one towards another; and they thirst after blood and revenge continually" (Moroni 9:3–5). Mormon goes on to describe his people, whom he had loved and served, as "without order and without mercy . . . brutal, sparing none" and as "delighting . . . in everything save that which is good . . . without principle, [and] past feeling" (Moroni 9:19–21). He closes his tragic commentary by telling his son that he cannot recommend his people unto God (see Moroni 9:18–21). The path for such behavior is, and always has been, the same: spiritual, physical, and ultimately literal destruction.

REVIVING YOUR SOUL

The secret to avoiding such hazards is, as on the single track, using our gifts and keeping open and positive communication. Prayer is the positive communication I speak of here. Prayer does two important things for us. First, it allows us to reach out to God and share our hopes, our fears, and our plans in a very personal way. It allows us to recognize and express gratitude as well as seek assistance. Through it, we can organize our priorities, commit ourselves, and report our progress.

Second, it allows us to throw the gates of communication wide open, as we meditate, study, and ponder, to receive pure and personal guidance in return. The key to this step, assuming we have done what is necessary to recognize such guidance, is that we must be so open that we are willing to accept whatever response we receive, even if it is not the answer we wanted or not in our desired timing. Such active communication, practiced with regularity, brings peace and strength. It allows us to better understand soul-saving principles and make additional strides in gaining an eternal perspective while dealing with life's many challenges. The bonus that comes over time is that we become more humble and open, which allows us to get to know not just the written word of God but the Author Himself.

In regularly seeking our Father in sincere, faith-filled, open-minded, humble prayer, we are promised that we will always have His Spirit to be with us, that we will receive gifts as necessary to accomplish the work we are placed here to do, and that we will, through such blessings be able to stand and not faint when faced by even the gravest tests of this mortal existence. Truly the Lord spoke to us all when He said, "And it is my will that you shall humble yourselves before me, and obtain this blessing by your diligence and humility and the prayer of faith. And inasmuch as you are diligent and humble, and exercise the prayer of faith, behold . . . I shall send means unto you for your deliverance" (Doctrine and Covenants 104:79–80). As a personal promise, He added, "Ask, and it shall be given you; seek, and ye shall find; knock, and it shall be opened unto you: For every one that asketh receiveth; and he that seeketh findeth; and to him that knocketh it shall be opened" (Matthew 7:7–8). And further, "He that humbleth himself shall be exalted" (Luke 14:11).

This is one of the most difficult principles for youth and young adults to appreciate. There is real power in prayer; as James tells us, "the effectual fervent prayer of a righteous man availeth much" (James 5:16). Too often our youth and young adults (and many adults for that matter) view prayer as a passing comment directed into space as we are on our way to somewhere else.

Would you call your father on his birthday, say a few words with little thought, and then hang up? Of course not. But to some, this passes as prayer. God, of course, hears such words, but if the person praying doesn't care to approach their Heavenly Father with a sincere effort and an attempt at real communication and a meaningful relationship, they will reap what they sow, which is practically nothing. Don't jump to conclusions here thinking that God will engage in a "tit for tat" and refuse to respond out of offense. God always responds. But if we choose not to pay attention or don't really seek anything, we will not hear Him, nor will we recognize His hand in our lives. Prayer is powerful, it can produce blessings in our lives, and it can save and heal us. But if we deaden our souls to God, how can we hear His response or recognize His answer when it comes?

As we keep the lines of communication with our Heavenly Father open—with regular, fervent prayer and active listening—we quicken our spiritual senses and enlighten our minds, thus allowing us to avoid unnecessary difficulty. The added bonus is that in spite of challenges that will still arise along the way, regular prayer keeps us close to Him and allows us to maintain a positive, faith-filled perspective. We will become better able to overcome destructive traps, some of which lead to anger, bitterness, and hate.

7

Sometimes You Hit the Rock Anyway

No matter how experienced you are on the trail or how conditioned you may be, bad things can still happen. They can happen even if you've done everything right, and they can have minor or major results. I remember riding up a particularly tricky portion of the trail. It is an uphill climb of perhaps fifty to seventy-five feet, and it's almost always wet and slick because a spring trickles down the path. I was riding with a friend and got to the left of my usual line. There was a large rock with a cradle in front of it that caught and stopped my front wheel immediately. I continued flying and landed hard, cutting my leg, and I was left bloody, dazed, and embarrassed. I lay there gathering my wits, and my friend rode above to make sure the path was clear and safe. After some first aid to stop the bleeding, checking the various bruises and abrasions, and realizing again how thankful I was for my helmet, we continued.

On another occasion I was headed down the trail alone, about a half mile below Big Rock, pedaling on an outside turn portion of the trail. There's a tendency among bikers to point your toes slightly downward as you pedal, and I was doing so. There was a flat-sided rock facing me, sticking up a mere three inches from the trail floor, and my left toe caught the flat side. Since my toes were in a toe-basket on each pedal, it flexed my bike frame and literally catapulted me and the bike to the right, through some six-foot-high oak, and into space. I didn't come to a stop until my bike and I hit the slope about twenty feet below the trail and rolled another eighty feet down a steep rock fall. Lying at the bottom, I looked up and realized the incline was very steep, and there was no way out except to climb back up to the trail. Again, I had my helmet on and was well-clothed, so abrasions and bruises were the extent of my injuries. My bike also was miraculously unscathed. It took twenty minutes of inching my bike, and then my body, a few feet at a time and hanging on to tree branches to get back to the top.

The rock is still there, and I have passed over it hundreds of times since. Every single time, I think about what happened and what I learned from it. (And by the way, I have never since pointed my toes on that portion of the trail!)

Sticks and Stones Do Break Your Bones

If you're going to be out in the world, bad things will occasionally happen. We were not sent here to live in a protected bubble, and God neither causes nor protects us from everything. Mountain biking is no different. While riding with two of my sons and one of my grandsons recently, we elected to ride a popular local "flow trail" near where we live. A flow trail is one where there are usually narrow wooden bridges, large roller-coaster-style paths built up sharp hills, and steep, high-banked, sharp turns. The 2.5-mile access trail ride up from the parking lot was challenging but not overwhelming. We arrived at the top full of enthusiasm, where we had our choice of several flow trails with varying levels of difficulty. Both the ride up and the flow trail down were fairly technical and definitely not for the novice rider. However, for those like me—who realize that I'm only one good crash away from feeling like I'm eighty years old—there are ways to ride downhill in a lower-impact way.

My boys and grandson are still young and fit enough to think they're immortal and were enjoying the thrills and jumps. We rode up the mountain and rolled or raced down twice, and then we decided

CHAPTER 7: SOMETIMES YOU HIT THE ROCK ANYWAY

we'd do it one last time. It's always the "one last time" of pushing your luck that should be avoided. We decided to try for a record time going up the access trail. There's a spot where there are two rocks jutting up and only enough room for your bike tire in between. I had my first fall on the third upward ride in that spot. I let out a loud, surprised howl as I went down, and one of my sons heard it and raced back to see if I needed help. He helped me get going again with only a few scrapes and a cut or two. I appreciated the assistance, and we continued to the top, not realizing that the next few minutes would change the day dramatically.

At the top, my sons and grandson chose to ride the more challenging route down, while I chose one that was challenging but more familiar. About halfway down, I noticed that the two routes paralleled, and I saw one of my sons and grandson speeding along the upper trail. I kept riding and then heard a familiar voice from the upper trail calling out "Dad!" with urgency. I stopped immediately and looked up to see my other son walking his bike.

"Is everything okay?" I asked.

"I had a pretty bad crash," he replied. "Do you think I can make it down to your trail?"

"Sure," I said, pointing out a path through the oak brush.

He explained he had come up over a high roller jump with a rock jutting out the top and attempted to jump, but his back tire caught on the rock, flipping him completely over forward. I have done that kind of flip on the trail before and know it can cause serious injury and often shock.

"I landed on my ribs and arm," he said. "I think I broke my elbow."

I had no idea that the same son who was there for me just a few minutes before would so soon afterward need me to be there for him. It was a tender mercy that I was a mere thirty feet away on the lower trail. Such events are rarely coincidental.

The toughest part of mountain biking is when you have a tough accident and you need to try to get down the hill as best as you can. My son traversed the brush to my trail and tentatively started down, with me following to help if necessary. His arm was already swelling and he was in serious pain. We made it to the bottom, and my other son and grandson helped him load his bike and pack everything up so he could drive home. As soon as he got home, his wife took him directly to the hospital where he discovered he had broken his arm just above the elbow and cracked a rib. His mountain biking hobby was obviously interrupted, and he and his wife have already decided that he is grounded from future flow trails and X-games.

We never know when our lives will be disrupted. We can plan, act prudently and responsibly, try to use good judgment, and follow safety rules and advice, but stuff often happens anyway. It does no good to beat yourself up, point fingers in blame, or sit there on the trail and feel sorry for yourself. There's always a way through the difficulty. My son was riding with others, and that was smart. He realized he was well enough to get down and did so quickly, on a safer route, while his adrenaline was still pumping. He sought out professional help and was able to quickly start recovering.

The key is never to dwell on the question "Why me?" It's better to do what you can in the moment, to use the resources you have at hand, and to get help. Then later we can ask, "What did God want me to learn from that experience?" This is taking responsibility. It's one of the most important principles of life and the gospel. Taking responsibility happens well before any good or bad event envelops you on the path.

Taking Responsibility Empowers You

As the preceding story illustrates, there are times when you can't avoid a large root, log, or rock. Frequently, it's possible to hop or roll over them with a slight loss of momentum and no harm done. Other times, as described above, the result is more severe, and on rare occasions, tragedy can occur. We can approach such experiences positively by attempting to learn from them and perhaps be a bit wiser in the future. To experience such growth, we must take responsibility for our role in whatever happens. This empowers us to further progress. It can also prevent the recurrence of a nasty mishap. Cursing the root or rock certainly won't change its behavior.

Refusal to accept responsibility for our actions hampers spiritual progress in two ways. First, it sets us up as helpless victims rather than empowered children of God. By blaming and expending energy to

Chapter 7: Sometimes You Hit the Rock Anyway

displace guilt for what happens to us, we reinforce in our hearts that it's not our fault—we had nothing to do with it and are victims. We can even feel as if we were simply innocent bystanders. But if we had nothing to do with it, how can we avoid it again? Where will we be "innocently standing" next time when a comet drops from the sky? We are helpless, powerless, and eventually hopeless. Our life becomes one of continual offense, unfairness, and defeat. It can destroy our faith in God and our hope for a better future because we tell ourselves the lie that we are not the ones who can make a difference.

Second, it disallows learning. Why? Because it's not our responsibility. Rather, it's the circumstance—something or someone else. Because we had nothing to do with it, we cannot overcome it. Therefore, there's nothing to learn unless we choose to become paranoid about all interactions. We become victims just waiting for the next calamity of life to befall us. Some even become obsessed with watching for the next time life will take advantage of them, and when it doesn't happen, they imagine an event or offense. Others are attracted to cultures that reinforce the idea that life is one long horrible trial, or the worse they suffer, the better off they'll be in the next life. They seek out or manufacture gratuitous suffering. Still others manufacture a cult of fear in themselves and in others over whom they have influence in a vain and selfish attempt to gain comfort through control over their own lives and the lives of others. This manufactured fear feeds on the exclusion of people, places, and activities they believe are part of the offense, and in a misguided effort to protect themselves, they create their own prison.

I remember a young lady who would not participate in religious observance because she had been offended. She felt that the local congregation had ignored her at an important time in her life. She finally came back years later, and those in the congregation responded with love and attention. Unfortunately, she was offended again because she received too much attention and it made her uncomfortable.

There's another individual I know who has described his life as one long string of faultless misadventures: losing jobs, abdicating parental responsibilities, and choosing not to pay obligations that are due to the government and lenders. This attitude left him in a deep emotional and financial hole. In addition, disengaging his association with family and children left him with little to live for, he believes. Yet through it all, he continues to make the same thinking errors that place him again and again in a position to fail. Why doesn't he see it?

Because he's a firm believer that life is against him, there is little he can do, and it's not his fault. What reason then is there to change behavior? The real tragedy is not what he has done to himself but what he has done to one of his sons who has bought into his father's arguments that "Life is unfair, so why try?" This fine young man in turn ceased making an effort to better his life and sunk into endless online computer gaming. Several have attempted to provide counsel to the father, but when someone slides so deeply into victimization and self-identified helplessness, they are simply unable to respond. Withdrawal and isolation do not make the demands of the world go away. Making up a pretend set of rules about how life should operate to suit you doesn't change things as they really are, and manipulating others into being loyal to your self-destructive cause only adds to the spiritual body count.

In today's latter-day era, we often hear some of the same arguments for not caring about the future that were heard in Paul and Peter's day. It's the ultimate cop-out that throws the Savior Himself under the bus. The argument focuses on the great calamities in the modern world and the admonitions to watch for the signs of the times that herald the Second Coming of Christ. They focus on every event in the heavens and on earth, every rumor and tumult and widespread illness, as being the beginning of the end. Whether this is true or not, it doesn't usually inspire people to prepare spiritually or temporally. It results in them losing motivation to seek a career, work to better their situation, or strengthen their family. I have heard more than once the statement "Why should I get a better job or improve my situation? It's all going to end next year [or fill in the date] anyway." Our best course is never to sit under a large plant like Jonah and wait for everything to be destroyed (see Jonah 4:5–6). It is to do the Lord's work with all our heart, might, mind, and strength until He comes (see Doctrine and Covenants 4: 1–4). Then we may find that He is familiar to us because we have become more like Him (see Doctrine and Covenants130:1; 1 John 3:2).

CHAPTER 7: SOMETIMES YOU HIT THE ROCK ANYWAY

Jacob described the inability of the children of Israel to follow God in a way that sounds hauntingly contemporary:

> The Spirit speaketh the truth and lieth not. Wherefore, it speaketh of things as they really are, and of things as they really will be; wherefore, these things are manifested unto us plainly. . . .
>
> But behold, the Jews were a stiffnecked people; and they despised the words of plainness . . . and sought for things that they could not understand. Wherefore, because of their blindness, which blindness came by looking beyond the mark, they must needs fall; for God hath taken away his plainness from them, and delivered unto them many things which they cannot understand, because they desired it. And because they desired it God hath done it, that they may stumble. (Jacob 4:13–14)

Nephi further illustrated this point in describing his mournful feelings for those he called wicked, ignorant, and stiffnecked: "For behold, they will not search knowledge, nor understand great knowledge, when it is given unto them in plainness, even as plain as word can be" (2 Nephi 32:7).

The gospel is not difficult to understand, nor is it mysterious. It's a message of love and kindness toward others, combined with respect, appreciation, and love of God. Biblical writers, prophets, and the Savior Himself spoke plainly of the path and the critical truths we must learn and follow to return to our Father's kingdom. Jesus taught, "If ye continue in my word, then are ye my disciples indeed; And ye shall know the truth, and the truth shall make you free" (John 8:31–32).

DISCERNING TRUTH FROM FABLE

That seems clear enough. However, the world is full of noise, counterfeits, and appealing but empty substitute paths. How can we identify the truth that will make us free? Paul saw our day and prophesied, "For the time will come when they will not endure sound doctrine; but after their own lusts shall they heap to themselves teachers, having itching ears; And they shall turn away their ears from the truth, and shall be turned unto fables" (2 Timothy 4:3–4). And Amos prophesied, "Behold, the days come, saith the Lord God, that I will send a famine in the land, not a famine of bread, nor a thirst for water, but of hearing the words of the Lord: And they shall wander from sea to sea, and from the north even to the east, they shall run to and fro to seek the word of the Lord, and shall not find it" (Amos 8:11–12).

How do we discern truth from fable and famine from feast? We continue in His word with patience, diligence, and faith. This is what Caleb and Joshua did when they were sent by Moses to scout out Canaan. The other scouts returned and spoke of a land rich with milk and honey but stated, "We be not able to go up against the people; for they are stronger than we. . . . In it are men of a great stature. . . . There we saw the giants . . . and we were in our own sight as grasshoppers" (Numbers 13:31–33). But Caleb responded in faith and said, "Let us go up at once, and possess it; for we are well able to overcome it" (Numbers 13:30). Joshua and Caleb also admonished the people to "rebel not ye against the Lord, neither fear ye the people of the land. . . . The Lord is with us: fear them not" (Numbers 14:9).

It's tempting to sink deeper into the trap by manufacturing or manipulating ever greater real or imagined failures ("fables") to feed the demands of self-pity and helplessness. Why does this happen? There are at least two reasons. First, it's uncomfortable to take responsibility, even though it usually is less so than we fear, and the duration of difficulty is shorter than imagined. However, the easier path can appear initially to be playing the victim or ignoring our own responsibility in the matter. One of the issues here is often insecurity in the position taken and eroded self-value. The "victim" can sometimes be seen attempting to manipulate others to their side to gain comfort or reinforcement for a behavior which, in their heart, they know is a sham. Later, more pronounced behavior can then be driven by increasing insecurity, and campaigning often ensues. Children are often the targets of this as they become co-opted into the transgression through unwittingly enabling the parental campaigner by giving in to pressure to pick sides and demonstrate loyalty through appearing to support the influencer's abusive behavior. Sadly, the campaigner then uses these children caught in the middle by placing blame for his or her own behavior upon the children by professing that he or she did nothing to influence them and that they made their own choices.

CHAPTER 7: SOMETIMES YOU HIT THE ROCK ANYWAY

I spoke with a young man years ago who had turned his back on organized religion because he felt they were telling him he had to be perfect (see Matthew 5:48; 3 Nephi 12:48). His conclusion was "I just don't see any practical application for religion in my life." Today he is a wonderful, faith-filled father and righteous man.

Another young man I know with the same concerns looks back and is now saddened because he feels ashamed that he spent so much effort trying to please others and become perfect (in his own eyes) instead of focusing on what God's will was and trying his best to follow it.

Neither the Lord nor The Church of Jesus Christ of Latter-day Saints, nor any Christian church with which I have come in contact, teaches that we must perfect ourselves. Of course, there are times when individuals or teachers or even some leaders may say something that could be taken that way, but only if one ignores the rest of the body of teachings and the gospel. In fact, the scripture "be ye therefore perfect" is translated in the Bible itself as "complete" rather than "perfect." The teachings of Jesus make it clear that we become perfect by striving to do our best and engage in sincere repentance along the way. Then the Savior's Atonement (grace) makes up the difference to fill the gap. This young man understood this, but it didn't fit his self-imposed narrative, so this inconvenient truth was set aside. The danger always is that if you have this impossible standard for yourself, you also probably apply it to others. The result often is offense or disappointment, which can impact future participation. It might be one of the greatest miracles of this earth life that Heavenly Father has been able to accomplish so much of His plan with such imperfect people.

Elder Jeffrey R. Holland spoke to this subject with firmness during the October 2024 general conference when he pled with all of us:

Down through history many have simplified, even trivialized our image of Him and His witness of who He was. They have reduced His righteousness to mere prudishness, His justice to mere anger, His mercy to mere permissiveness. We must not be guilty of such simplistic versions of Him that conveniently ignore teachings we find uncomfortable. . . .

There is a force in the universe determined to oppose *every good thing* you try to do. . . .

We stay the course with the true Church of Christ. Why? Because as with our Redeemer, we signed on for the whole term—not ending with the first short introductory quiz but through to the final exam. The joy in this is that the Headmaster gave us all open-book answers *before the course began*. Furthermore, we have a host of tutors who remind us of these answers at regular stops along the way. But of course, none of this works if we keep cutting class.

"Whom seek ye?" With all our hearts we answer, "Jesus of Nazareth."[19]

WHY ORGANIZING A CHURCH WAS SO IMPORTANT TO THE LORD'S PLAN AND OUR SALVATION

A close examination of the scriptures and the Lord's establishment of a Church deserves the question of not *whether* He established a Church but *why*. There is little question that an organization was established because God knew we could not make it alone. We need each other. Everything around us testifies of that in every aspect of life. When a job needs to be done, it's almost always easier with help. When a person is depressed or downtrodden, they seek out others to help bear the burden. God is not somehow the only one who couldn't figure this out.

He banded together a group of followers and counseled them to serve each other and administer to each other. He established this society in a way such that it was organized and divinely guided. The need has not changed. In fact, it may be greater now than ever before. The fact that God has been able to do this with imperfect people in a world where many other institutions have lost their way and become corrupted makes it an even greater miracle. It turns out that organizing a church that provides a place where well-meaning individuals can serve and uplift each other helps the giver just as much as the receiver.

The Lord Himself counseled us to remember that even the smallest acts can make a difference: "Be not weary in well-doing, for ye are laying the foundation of a great work. And out of small things proceedeth that which is great. Behold, the Lord requireth the heart and a willing mind; and the willing and obedient shall eat the good of

---

19. Jeffrey R. Holland, "I Am He," *Liahona*, Nov. 2024.

the land . . . in these last days" (Doctrine and Covenants 64:33–34). "Inasmuch as ye have done it unto one of the least of these my brethren, ye have done it unto me" (Matthew 25:40). There seems to be no question that service and ministering are a big deal to God. They should be a big part of our lives too. It only happens when we do it together.

Satan's Various Excuses to Sidestep Responsibility

Second, getting us to refuse to take responsibility for our actions is one of Satan's most effective tools and has been from the beginning. Let's look at a few examples of common excuses mankind has used throughout history and view them in a true light as important tools in Satan's workshop.

I am not responsible for my actions because . . .

- There is no God and therefore no one to be accountable to. Therefore, God's law cannot exist, and if there's no law, the concept of sin is false. Finally, there is no consequence, for there is no sin.
- There is a God, but I'm saved, perfect, or chosen; He is now in control of my life. Therefore, my acts are no longer my own. Sinful acts cannot be attributed to me.
- There is a God, but fate controls everything. Therefore, there can be no personal accountability because my acts are all predetermined.
- There is a God, but He's a disinterested entity with more important things to do, and what happens here is of no consequence—we're on our own. Nothing I do matters to Him, so why bother?
- It's not my fault. I was born with certain genetic predispositions that require that I act or control my acts in a certain way, or God made a mistake when He put me in this body. It is unavoidable; I have no choice.
- My environment is responsible—my circumstances, upbringing, particular disadvantages or hardships, and so on. These have controlled my acts.

- I ingested a substance that unexpectedly removed my ability to control my acts. The substance was therefore responsible.
- I wasn't prepared or paying attention, I forgot, or nobody told me, so I didn't know what I was responsible for. How can I be responsible?
- Someone told me to or made me do it, or I was simply following orders or directions.
- Everybody does it, so I can too. It's not my fault.
- I am nothing and of no consequence, I have no value and am invisible to others, so what I do doesn't matter. Why should I try at all?
- What I do only affects me, so there should be no consequences.
- The end justifies the means. Life has been unfair, and I am therefore entitled to get whatever I want to balance the scales.

In a limited way and in certain circumstances, some of these may be justifiable. For example, we cannot be responsible for something we didn't know and didn't have an opportunity to learn. However, we cannot sidestep responsibility because we deny or refuse to accept or seek out the understanding that is available. Regardless of the craftiness or seductiveness of these arguments or whether they are up to date, popular, or hip, the result is the same. Satan seeks to deceive us and have us avoid responsibility for our actions. Those caught in this trap seek to justify any behavior, just as Cain, King Saul, Sherem, Korihor, and Pilate did (see Genesis 4:1–16; 1 Samuel 15:24–25; Jacob 7:18; Alma 30:52–53; Matthew 27:24). Unfortunately, they often draw others with them.

Taking Responsibility Draws You Closer to God

Taking responsibility for our acts involves all the best Christlike qualities. It requires courage, repentance, and forgiveness. It builds trust in the Lord and faith and allows us to love God and our fellow men more fully. It allows us to reach out to our Heavenly Father through a veil of tears and feel His loving arms enfold us and learn to more fully understand the grace embodied in our Savior Jesus Christ's great sacrifice. It gives us power to overcome trials, to learn, and to become wiser. But most of all, it's a practice field for the exercise of

CHAPTER 7: SOMETIMES YOU HIT THE ROCK ANYWAY

our freedom to choose and the divine concept of forgiveness of others. How? Because accepting responsibility opens the door to improvement through contrite repentance. As we pedal up this difficult path, we gain understanding and insight as to the need for the Savior's Atonement and a greater appreciation of the incomprehensible gift of love that it is.

Forgiveness is the opportunity to exercise some small portion of the Atonement toward others. Paul defines this love of others as that which the Savior has for us and refers to this as the ultimate Christlike characteristic: "Charity suffereth long, and is kind; charity envieth not; charity vaunteth not itself, is not puffed up, Doth not behave itself unseemly, seeketh not her own, is not easily provoked, thinketh no evil; Rejoiceth not in iniquity, but rejoiceth in the truth; Beareth all things, believeth all things, hopeth all things, endureth all things. Charity never faileth. . . . And now abideth faith, hope, charity, these three; but the greatest of these is charity" (I Corinthians 13:4–8; 13). Mormon refers to this as the pure love of Christ: "Wherefore, my beloved brethren, pray unto the Father with all the energy of heart, that ye may be filled with this love . . . that when he shall appear we shall be like him . . . that we may be purified even as he is pure" (Moroni 7:48).

By taking responsibility for our lives and actions, we choose to empower ourselves. This enables growth and allows us to develop an appreciation of the Savior's great sacrifice as we turn to Him and feel His love. It leads us in the path of developing Christlike characteristics that will enrich our lives and uplift all those around us, the greatest of which is charity.

8
Map Reading: The Big Picture

ANY MOUNTAIN RIDER IS WISE TO PICK UP A MAP OR READ ONE OF the many online trail guides prior to taking on a new trail. It is not difficult on most popular trails to even find a video. The more familiar you are with the trail, the less likely you are to get lost or be surprised by terrain that may be too technical or steep. A map, although lacking specific terrain detail, provides an important overview of the intended trip. However, a map is no substitute for an experienced, on-the-ground guide. I remember my first downhill ride on Baldy Mountain at the Sun Valley ski resort. I took my wife and four of our sons, anticipating an enjoyable afternoon of coasting and rolling. I am a map hound and studied a copy of the trail map and carried it with me on the ride. Unfortunately, the map was not sufficiently detailed to help us make better decisions along the way that would have improved our level of enjoyment.

The trip up the mountain via the ski lift was enjoyable and beautiful. The trail down did have some unexpected uphill portions where some in our group walked their bikes, but we stayed together and had a great time. But just as we were beginning to descend the Warm Springs switchbacks, we came to a fork in the trail. Instead of continuing down the Warm Springs side, which looked a bit steeper on the map because of the frequent switchbacks, I led us on a trail back to the Baldy Face. This was a mistake because it included a long traverse uphill. Everyone was tired by this point; pushing a bike uphill is not a relaxing hike. After about half a mile, we came to some nice riding on a jeep trail, which everyone enjoyed. The jeep trail turned into a cat track that went straight down an extremely steep ski slope with loose rocks for about a hundred yards, ending at one of the ski lifts. We walked our bikes carefully down the hill and took the lift the rest of the way down to the car. We had an enjoyable ride, but had I been more familiar with the trail, I would have known that the Warm Springs side would have been much more enjoyable. I took my son and son-in-law that way the following year and learned the truth for myself. It was great, much faster, and went right down to the parking lot.

Understanding the bigger picture while still picking up the critical details is a must during our journey through this life. I had the opportunity to teach an adult Sunday School class for a few years and came across a suggested activity that played out better than expected during one of the sessions. On this occasion, we were talking about the big picture overview of the fulness of the gospel and how it helps us have an eternal perspective.

Solving Puzzles

We enjoy doing puzzles together as a family and had recently completed a 1,000-piece puzzle of the well-known painting of Jesus knocking at the door. I put all the pieces into three Ziploc bags and placed them out of view of the class. I had one puzzle piece in my pocket that was featureless and black. At the beginning of the session, I asked a good-natured friend of mine if he would help me with a little demonstration. As things got underway, I called my friend to the front and asked him if he thought he was pretty good at doing puzzles. He explained they didn't do them that often but that he thought he could handle one all right. I then pulled out the black puzzle piece and handed it to him, telling him it was a true and accurate piece of one of our family's puzzles.

CHAPTER 8: MAP READING: THE BIG PICTURE

I asked him to take as long as he wanted to examine it and then to tell me what picture the puzzle piece was from. He looked at the featureless piece for a moment and smiled as chuckles came from the class. "I can't do it," he said. I asked why. He said that he needed the rest of the pieces of the puzzle and then he could answer. As he gave a satisfied glance at the rest of the class, I pulled out the three Ziploc bags from their hiding place, tossed them on the table, and said, "Okay, here are the rest of the pieces—now tell me what the picture looks like." He looked at me blankly as the group broke into laughter and simply said, "I need the picture."

With the visual example fresh in everyone's mind, I allowed my friend to return to his seat and explained that there are several necessary steps to complete the puzzle. Only then will the entire picture become clear and complete. Here are the principles we discussed as they pertain to the puzzle and the gospel.

- Many people have some true pieces of the gospel, and some have many true pieces of the gospel. In fact, it may be possible to have all the true pieces, but like the bags of puzzle pieces on the table, it still doesn't help complete the picture. To successfully complete the puzzle, you must have a sufficiently detailed map or picture as well as all the pieces.
- Any new puzzle comes with a picture of what it looks like when finished, which is critical to making any progress. This is a must in understanding your overall objective and how everything fits together.
- The complete gospel of Jesus Christ has all the pieces as well as the means to guide us in putting them together properly (see chapter 4).
- When putting together a large puzzle, you're most likely to succeed by following these steps:
  - Place the picture of the finished puzzle (sometimes on the box top) where it's visible and can be referred to. Then lay out all the puzzle pieces.
  - Start with the edges so you can set the boundaries. This allows you to understand the limits of the puzzle.

- Build the areas that have easily identifiable features like faces, animals, trees, or buildings. This helps fill in the puzzle, but there will still be gaps.
- The puzzle then becomes harder as the solid colors and those with unclear features are worked on. One must look at shading, slight differences in hue, and puzzle piece shape. There is always a little trial and error, but the puzzle will come together.

The Full Picture

The fulness of the gospel has been revealed through ancient and modern-day prophets. Studying the gospel by the Spirit (see 2 Peter 1:18–21; Moroni 10:3–5) allows us to set the boundaries for truth and separate it from the adversary's counterfeit worldly teachings. As we learn "precept upon precept, line upon line" (1 Nephi 28:30), our knowledge grows and we are better able to pull together aspects of the gospel that are easily identified.

These may include basic doctrines, principles, personal obligations, and the framework of commandments and covenants we have been given. As we continue to grow through obedience and faithfulness, we then are increasingly able to fill in the remainder of the gospel pieces through endurance amidst life's experiences as our minds are enlightened by the Holy Ghost. Understanding some principles more fully requires the test of time and exposure to challenges as well as prayerful study and obedience.

Among these are principles for which we often pay a price. They include repentance, forgiveness, obedience, love, long-suffering, patience, and the interconnection of faith, hope and charity. Throughout a faithfully lived life, full of service to others, we fill in the gaps and grow to understand the entire picture. We can see as we are seen, know as we are known, and ultimately be changed into the image of the Lord from glory to glory by the Spirit (see 1 Corinthians 13:12; 2 Corinthians 3:18) and receive a fulness of His grace (see Doctrine and Covenants 76:94).

The real tragedy happens when those who have strived so hard to obtain a clearer picture of the puzzle choose by their actions or

CHAPTER 8: MAP READING: THE BIG PICTURE

behavior to intentionally discard pieces or the overall guiding picture. Over time, this degrades their ability to complete the puzzle and, in some cases, recall what the full picture looked like in the first place.

Let's take an example of what missing one important piece of a puzzle can do to mankind's understanding of the big picture. Few in the world have a real appreciation of the concept of Jesus Christ's Atonement and Resurrection. Careful study of the word of God gives us insight into this important principle. Think for a moment of the confusion that reigns because most of the world is missing just this one piece of the gospel puzzle. How can someone have any clear conviction about where we go after this life, the concept of why bad things happen to good people, why there is suffering, the worth of individuals even if they're sinners, the concept of a loving versus a vengeful God, or the purpose behind why we're here at all? It is understandable why, for example, so many in the world would be confused about the purpose of this life, the importance of marriage and family, the need for continuing guidance from God, their relationship with God, the true character of the Father and Son, and countless other lifesaving and comfort-giving doctrines.

WHY PROPHETS ARE NEEDED

On March 25, 2010, *Newsweek* reported on a series of surveys completed regarding the concept of resurrection. Eighty percent of Americans surveyed said they believed in the concept of heaven. However, the writer reported that there was little agreement on what, if anything, happens there. In fact, referencing several surveys, *Newsweek* reported that only 26 percent of Americans believed in a physical resurrection, while 30 percent said they believed in reincarnation, and 21 percent of those who professed to be Christian believed in reincarnation.[20] This "intellectual flabbiness"[21] can hardly be avoided when so much of the real picture is unclear and the adversary is working to obscure it further by telling us that the events described in the scriptures are not actual events but rather metaphors or

---

20. Lisa Miller, "The Christian Mystery of Physical Resurrection," *Newsweek*, March 24, 2010, http://www.newsweek.com/id/235418.

21. Miller, "The Christian Mystery."

symbolism. Modern-day religionists provide little assistance by side-stepping answers with the defense that these are great mysteries that man was not meant to understand or by simply buying into pop-culture explanations.

Human nature then takes over as individuals start choosing what principles fit into their lives and call it spiritualism. What is this? It is, in fact, the equivalent of tossing God to the curb and making themself the god of their own world. It's a lazy and narcissistic counterfeit because the basic assumption is that if God were really as smart as me, He would have figured this out long ago. It may work just fine for short periods of smooth sailing, but it will not and cannot save or protect and leads to nowhere.

Amos prophesied that a time would come when the Lord would "send a famine in the land, not a famine of bread, nor a thirst for water, but of hearing the words of the Lord: And they shall wander from sea to sea, and from the north even to the east, they shall run to and fro to seek the word of the Lord, and shall not find it" (Amos 8:11–12). Is not this an accurate description of modern society?

Amos further counseled us that "surely the Lord God will do nothing, but he revealeth his secret unto his servants the prophets" (Amos 3:7). Are we to believe that God's work is done and that He currently does nothing for humankind? We certainly are not at the point in society where there are no problems. The Savior expanded on this important concept by clarifying to Peter that the rock that is revelation did exist and must continue if the gates of hell are not to prevail (see Matthew 16:17–18). To be clear, this reference means that for His organization and the gospel to prevail and continue, it must be built upon a foundation of revelation through a prophet as well as the right of each individual to receive personal revelation for guidance in their own life (see Ephesians 2:20; 4:11–14). Clearly we have not arrived at a "unity of the faith" (Ephesians 4:14); therefore, this should continue to be the case. There is no question that we certainly could use it. Only this continuing access and communication with God through the Holy Ghost, combined with sincere study of the word of God, allows us to complete key sections of the full gospel picture.

Throughout history, good men and women have continued to rely upon God's revelatory guidance and providence and seek to

CHAPTER 8: MAP READING: THE BIG PICTURE

understand His ongoing will. They have wondered at the confusion and distraction of mankind. In the year 1838, Ralph Waldo Emerson delivered an address before the senior class of the Cambridge University Divinity School. He said, "And it is my duty to say to you that the need was never greater of new revelation than now. . . . It is the office of a true teacher to show us that God is, not was; that He speaketh, not spake. . . . Men have come to speak of . . . revelation as somewhat long ago given and done, as if God were dead."[22]

God, of course, is not dead. But we would assign Him the attributes of a disinterested God whose work with us is finished, a mindless moviedom midi-chlorian force, or even a non-existent myth. Dr. Robert Gordon Sproul, president of the University of California from 1930 to 1958, described essentially the same condition in modern Christian churches as did Mr. Emerson a hundred years earlier:

> We have the peculiar spectacle of a nation, which to a limited extent practices Christianity without actively believing in Christianity. We are asked to turn to the church for enlightenment but when we do we find that the voice of the church is not inspired. The voice of the church today is the echo of our own voices. . . . The way out is the sound of a voice, not our voice. . . . It is the task of the pastors to hear this voice, cause us to hear it and tell us what it says. . . . Without it we are no more capable of saving the earth than we were capable of creating it in the first place.[23]

YOU CAN HEAR HIM: SPIRITUAL GPS

The Church of Jesus Christ of Latter-day Saints has engaged throughout its existence in just such an effort to teach all people how they can better hear and come unto Him. In 2020, during a time when great calamities faced the world, God counseled us through his prophet, President Russell M. Nelson, about the central importance of this principle. President Nelson shared:

---

22. Ralph Waldo Emerson, "The Divinity School Address by Ralph Waldo Emerson [July 15, 1838]," Age of the Sage, accessed Nov. 5, 2024, https://www.age-of-the-sage.org/emerson/the-divinity-school-address.html.

23. Quoted in Howard W. Hunter, "Spiritual Famine" *Ensign*, Jan. 1973, 64.

Repeatedly, past prophets have declared "great and marvelous things unto the people, which they did not believe." It is no different in our day. . . . Yet most people do *not* embrace these truths— either because they do not know where to look for them or because they are listening to those who do not have the whole truth or because they have rejected truth in favor of worldly pursuits. . . . However, messages from our Heavenly Father are strikingly different. He communicates simply, quietly, and with such stunning plainness that we cannot misunderstand Him.[24]

The adversary is clever. For millennia, he has been making good look evil and evil look good (see Isaiah 5:20). His messages tend to be loud, bold, and boastful.

"Regardless of where you live or what your circumstances are, the Lord Jesus Christ is *your* Savior, and God's prophet . . . is *your* prophet," President Nelson continued.[25] He also reminded us that "nothing shall be withheld" from the faithful (Doctrine and Covenants 121:28).

Modern automobiles have devices that utilize GPS technology (global positioning satellite). It includes helpful maps and directions for virtually anywhere we wish to travel. No more fumbling with fold-out maps or written directions—the computer voice gives us real-time guidance as needed until we arrive at our designated location. It's a great tool, especially for the directionally challenged. My family was discussing this miraculous technology once, and I asked two of my sons what the key benefit of the GPS device was in their opinion. They responded with the mapping application and the "it gets you where you want to go" answers, which are both important features. I, however, suggested that there was another feature that was more important, and without it, the mapping and destination capabilities would be useless. After a moment of questioning looks, I told them the most important and basic feature is that it tells you where *you* are at any given moment (with a small error factor).

Having a map and knowing your destination is meaningless if you don't know where you are on the map in relation to that destination.

---

24. Russell M. Nelson, "Hear Him," *Ensign* or *Liahona*, May 2020, 89.

25. Russell M. Nelson, "Hear Him," 88.

CHAPTER 8: MAP READING: THE BIG PICTURE

Therefore, with no place to begin, it is a meaningless instrument. However, because the GPS device automatically determines your location, all the other applications can run, and off you go.

Ever-growing clarity and understanding of the gospel requires ongoing location, position, and destination capability. This is found in the gift and direction of the Holy Ghost. It can tell you where you are in relation to where you need to be and how to get there. Continuing guidance is as critical to our spiritual progress as knowing where you are on the map. Because any movement spiritually, like when driving, changes your coordinates on the map, this guidance must be ongoing or else it becomes imperfect and potentially flawed. It's not uncommon to pick up an old map, for example, and attempt to use it on a long drive, only to discover that there are changes in the roads that are not reflected. God is not forgetful of us; He has not abandoned us during these troubled times. He is there still and ever ready to give you a response.

I have a son who's a pilot, and he explained that GPS only remains accurate because the United States Air Force has a staff that regularly adjusts and corrects errors that occur naturally in the global positioning satellites. Were this not ongoing every few weeks, GPS would very quickly become useless. Fine-tuning our ability to hear Him is just as critical.

Knowing that we lived with God before this life and that we made choices to come here is important. Knowing that this earth was created for our benefit to help us become the kind of people we must to return and live with our Father again—and that all of this is because of His love for us—tells us we're important. Understanding that we're not insignificant specks of sand in the universe but are valued sons and daughters of God Himself reinforces our eternal value. Understanding that He has not left us alone but has promised to provide continuing spiritual guidance to us directly, as well as His promise that there would continue to be prophets, gives us confidence to carry on.

The charge then is to avail ourselves of this promised direct access to our God in personal prayer and seek this promised personal revelation. Our further charge is to also seek out those who He promised would be the foundation of our faith, along with Jesus, who is the chief cornerstone in this day, and learn of them (see Ephesians 2:20).

This knowledge allows us greater perspective, just as a GPS and map do, so we don't become lost and disoriented.

The world is full of questions, and the revealed fulness of the gospel answers them. It provides a clear picture—an overall map. But our loving Father has not sent us out with a map and a picture and left us alone. He has provided a Comforter, even the Holy Ghost, as a daily guide through the detailed terrain of our individual path (see John 14:26; Doctrine and Covenants 75:10). He has, through Jesus Christ, provided an atoning sacrifice that we might overcome our mistakes and recover from taking a wrong turn. He has also provided the scriptures and continuing revelatory guidance so that we can become fully converted, strengthen each other, and develop selfless, Christlike love through serving each other (see Luke 22:32; John 15:12–13).

I remember one occasion visiting the home of an elderly sister to participate in giving her a blessing prior to her going to the hospital for a rather serious operation. Her daughter was present, and I had a feeling from the Spirit that she was burdened with something unspoken and also needed a blessing (see James 5:14–15). I asked if she would like one also. She answered, "I can't. I have things to work out." I felt an outpouring of God's love for her and witnessed to her of her Father in Heaven's love for her regardless of any mistakes she had made or whether she had paid any attention to Him over the past years.

I further pointed out that He was always there for her and that blessings were for all of us, flawed as we are, to strengthen us and let us know of our importance to Him. She again declined with the same words. I have thought much about the missing pieces in her life and how we can help her find and pull them together again. The Savior said of Himself, "I lay down my life for the sheep" (John 10:15) and "I am the resurrection, and the life" (John 11:25). His sheep are not just those who are doing all they can to be faithful; His flock includes us all, that we might not have to also suffer (see Doctrine and Covenants 19:16).

The Apostle James promised us, "If any of you lack wisdom, let him ask of God, that giveth to all men liberally, and upbraideth not; and it shall be given him" (James 1:5). Jesus also reiterated this promise Himself when He taught, "Ask, and it shall be given you; seek, and ye shall find; knock, and it shall be opened unto you: For every one that asketh receiveth; and he that seeketh findeth; and to him that knocketh it shall be opened" (Matthew 7:7–8).

The Lord, speaking to Oliver Cowdery, gave us great hope when He said:

Verily, verily, I say unto thee, blessed art thou for what thou hast done; for thou hast inquired of me, and behold, as often as thou hast inquired thou hast received instruction of my Spirit. If it had not been so, thou wouldst not have come to the place where thou art at this time.

Behold, thou knowest that thou hast inquired of me and I did enlighten thy mind. . . .

Yea, I tell thee, that thou mayest know that there is none else save God that knowest thy thoughts and the intents of thy heart. . . .

Verily, verily, I say unto you, if you desire a further witness, cast your mind upon the night that you cried unto me in your heart, that you might know concerning the truth of these things.

Did I not speak peace to your mind concerning the matter? What greater witness can you have than from God?

And now, behold, you have received a witness; for if I have told you things which no man knoweth have you not received a witness? . . .

Look unto me in every thought; doubt not, fear not. (Doctrine and Covenants 6:14–16, 22–23, 36)

Use the map we have been given to pull together the pieces of the most important picture in your life. As you move forward, continue to seek personal guidance from God to be sure of your position on that map and any approaching hazards. Know that you are loved and that there is always a hand there to lift you up if you will but look. He knows us and our situation and wants us to succeed.

9
A Sense of Humor
and a Good Pace

ONE ASPECT OF BIKING ON THE LOCAL TRAIL IS THAT IT'S USUALLY A positive social experience. People are friendly and encouraging. If you have a mechanical problem or mishap, others are quick to offer assistance. There are also usually a few friendly people at Big Rock with whom to chat. This makes the exertion and obstacles overcome along the way more pleasant. It's not uncommon to have another rider or two arrive at Big Rock feeling tired and worn. Some may even express frustration that the ride was much more difficult than anticipated. My response is usually to encourage them, make room for them on the bench, and give them a reminder that anyone who can sit on that bench on a Saturday morning has accomplished something worthwhile and should feel pretty good. It doesn't matter how long it took to get there.

As previously mentioned, mountain rides at a 5,000- to 7,000-foot elevation can present very different challenges depending on the weather. Some rides can be miserable with rain or snow. Others can be refreshing, like when there's a cool canyon breeze on a hot day. The Mueller Park Trail is quick to recover from heavy precipitation.

It dries out rapidly, although there are always a few lingering puddles and a couple of rather technical muddy slopes on the way to Big Rock.

A few years ago, I bundled up because it had recently rained, and it was still drizzling slightly for the first half of the ride. A small rivulet of water ran down the center of the track in many places. Because the trail has much undergrowth nearby and sometimes on it, it's not possible to avoid brushing against the water-laden branches and leaves. This will soak your clothes quickly. On this day, I expected such a result, so I layered up and wore an extra windbreaker. The ride was sloppy, muddy, and wet as I rode an out-and-back to Big Rock. By the time I got back to the trailhead, my entire front from head to toe was covered with splatters of mud and dirty water. I had no fender on my front tire, so I became a human mud flap. I must say that I was miserable and soaked through all my layers by the time I crossed the bridge to the parking lot.

As I stopped to consider my plight, I noticed an athletic-looking, college-aged woman who was preparing to start her ride. She couldn't have looked more out of place. She was dressed in a newly washed, white T-shirt and white sweats, with nice clean white socks and even white running shoes. Now, I know how difficult it is to get mud splatter stains out of white clothing, but I said nothing—and I didn't need to. She looked up at me, and I must have looked like something out of a 1950s "B" movie with the words "Swamp Thing" in the title. She simply said, "So . . . is it muddy up there on the trail today?" I was dumbfounded at a question that was easily answered with a glance. I hesitated a moment, considering how to respond, and then said, "Oh no, it's perfectly dry." We both broke out into roll-on-the-floor laughter. Suddenly looking like the inside of a fender didn't feel so terrible.

WHAT IS—AND IS NOT—HUMOR

A good sense of humor doesn't mean tearing down others or being crass, it doesn't require engaging in off-color stories or profanity, and it certainly doesn't include making light of sacred things. Such examples are, in fact, not humor at all. Life seems to present situations that give us opportunities to lighten our burdens and raise our spirits. A sense of humor is an art based in remaining cheerful and

CHAPTER 9: A SENSE OF HUMOR AND A GOOD PACE

obtaining and using the spiritual gift of finding joy and wonder along the path. The Lord reminded His disciples frequently that even in the most difficult times, they should "be of good cheer" (Matthew 14:27), and Paul teaches us that "God loveth a cheerful giver" (2 Corinthians 9:7). And even in the most daunting moments, we can remember the words of the Savior: "These things I have spoken unto you, that in me ye might have peace. In the world ye shall have tribulation: but be of good cheer; I have overcome the world" (John 16:33). "When thou art in tribulation, and all these things are come upon thee, even in the latter days, if thou turn to the Lord thy God, and shalt be obedient unto his voice; . . . he will not forsake thee" (Deuteronomy 4:30–31). The better we understand how valuable we are to our Heavenly Father, how much He has done for us, and how much He desires to bless us further, the easier it is to find enjoyment and maintain our cheerful outlook and wholesome sense of humor even during the darkest of times.

As my friends and I age, it seems there are an increasing number of spiritual and physical challenges in our lives. In our twenties, we talked about sports. Later, our conversations were about our children and families. Nowadays, it seems talk centers increasingly on what operations, aches, and maladies we have. (I know, it sounds pathetic to me too.) Some of these challenges can be overcome. Others require adjustments in behavior and lifestyle. A few are life-threatening, and there are those that break your heart. I recently visited a good friend in the hospital; he is now retired after thirty-six years as the local fire chief. He has been physically active but had experienced a series of disheartening medical setbacks since his retirement. On this occasion, he was facing an unexpected emergency caused by blood clots lodged in his lungs.

I was concerned that I would find him discouraged. Upon entering his space in the emergency room, I was greeted by a cheerful hello. We had an uplifting conversation, and I was impressed that he had maintained his positive outlook on life. We discussed his situation, and he and his sweet wife kept up a conversation back and forth that reminded me more of a relaxing Saturday afternoon on their back porch rather than sitting behind curtains in the ER. The high point was when he told of taking his oldest son (who is now a firefighter himself and arranged for the paramedics to transport his dad to the ER) to the fire station a number of years before. His son was young and very excited and enjoyed the day. However, on the ride home, he seemed disappointed. My friend recalled asking his son what was wrong, and the boy turned to his father and said, "Dad, I was hoping to see all the clowns you've always said you work with." We laughed, and it brightened all our spirits.

Enjoying the Ride Versus Getting Discouraged

The built-in calamities of life on this earth—and the very nature of growing older and having children who in turn grow and multiply—bring with them many situations and events that provide severe tests. Some approach life being wound so tightly that every little thing becomes big, and they have nothing left when something big actually occurs. I worked for many years in one of the most intense professions imaginable, that of investment banking. Pressure to perform was constant, competition was extreme, and expectations were always extraordinarily high. I watched as many of my peers' priorities became altered and their pace frenzied. It was tragic as so many good men and women fell by the wayside or were crushed under the mounting stress simply because they had not given sufficient place for faith and hope. Therefore, they took it all so seriously and could not allow themselves to enjoy the process. Worst of all, some were unable to laugh at themselves or their situation when that could have been the very best medicine. Of course, a person's occupation is important, as is their faith and family. But we cannot become so intense that we break ourselves against the challenges of life. I've found that a sense of humor, the ability to find that which is good and uplifting along the way, and keeping a healthy perspective about the trail and my priorities have made a big difference in my ability to endure.

What's the difference? Some have an ability to bring cheer regardless of the circumstances. Others are able to maintain a healthy and hopeful outlook because they've balanced their life. Yes, they may have stress in their jobs or due to family, health, faithfulness, or financial concerns, as do we all. But their focus on their family and their relationship with God, their understanding of the Savior's sacrifice for

CHAPTER 9: A SENSE OF HUMOR AND A GOOD PACE

them, and the blessings that come from giving to others are all critical to keeping life's stressors in perspective.

Years ago, my mother's next-door neighbor was a gentleman who had survived the Bataan Death March and years of captivity in Japanese prisoner of war camps during the Second World War. He wrote a book describing his experiences, and I was given a signed copy. He made this observation about those who survived the incomprehensible trials versus those who did not:

> It was a gut-wrenching experience when cleaning up after a death, to be watched by ten or fifteen pairs of glazed eyes and have someone say, "Lieutenant, you can do that for me tomorrow." I knew that it would happen. Most often the illness would be real, but sometimes it was just a case of giving up; the will to live had been lost. There was nothing more I could say or do to help, and I have lived with the frustration of that failure ever since. . . .
>
> There I learned another survival skill: the control of depression, perhaps more insidious and lethal than the diseases with which we were now so familiar. Everyone was affected by it to some degree, and it took a conscious and continuous effort to overcome. Never allow the overwhelming daily stress to obscure the ultimate goal. Immerse oneself in helping others where possible, realizing that in so doing personal psychological problems are minimized to the point that they are bearable. Search always for the bright side of any situation, even though its light may be very dim most of the time. This approach, partly deliberate and partly instinctive, was vital to the preservation of mental and physical stability. I could sense it in myself and observe it working for others, who almost always were the ones contributing to the general welfare of the camp.[26]

We don't have to look for extreme situations to find such strengths and weaknesses among us. The world today seems to be full of "can't do" attitudes. On one hand, pop culture seems to encourage us to do whatever feels good without any limits. On the other hand, when a person desires to make something of themselves or achieve some great benefit for mankind, the streets seem to be lined with crowds

---

26. Thomas R. Harrison, *Survivor: Memoir of Defeat and Captivity Bataan, 1942* (Western Epics, 1989), 164–65.

discouraging the effort. The public chants seem to be "It can't be done," "Don't waste your time," "We have to learn to lower our expectations," or simply "It's not worth all the effort." With so many easy diversions available that take no effort, learning, or commitment, it's tempting to avoid marriage, raising a family, adhering to standards and values, attempting to set and achieve goals or better your situation in life, face up to and correct problems you or those around you may have, or take virtually any action that could result in growth. The gospel of Jesus Christ is a "can do" philosophy. The Savior made it clear that nothing is impossible; anything can be accomplished as long as we work at it with God as part of our team (see Matthew 19:26; Mark 10:27; Luke 1:37; Luke 18:27).

Saints to Sinners

I remember riding a very long leg on the Saints to Sinners 520-mile relay race from Salt Lake City to Las Vegas. My relay assignment at that point was to ride south through Panguitch, Utah, and up into the Dixie National Forest to Panguitch Lake. Through the town was easy and flat, and then we began to rise into the mountains. The challenge was that there were seven different initial long upgrades that all appeared to flatten out but then immediately rose again into another climb. During these seven successive hills, it was easy to become discouraged and wonder if it would ever end. I decided to begin focusing on the short term instead of dwelling on the entire mountain. I started counting pedal rotations. I would count ten of them and then start over. This way, all I had to ever do was ten more. Of course, I counted to ten hundreds of times, but for some reason, it mattered less. Staying focused on a difficult, seemingly insurmountable mountain climb in very small segments kept my mind from focusing on more than it could handle. It also helped that I didn't know how many successive hills there were—ignorance can be helpful too sometimes.

The person who uses up all their energy fighting the hill with every rotation of the pedal is the perfect example of first-mile burnout. Life is not about who races ahead at the start; it's about getting to the goal prepared and ready to move on. The person who can maintain a positive outlook, and who takes time to learn the skills that will allow them to do so, will still be on the hill pumping long after others have turned around and headed back.

10

Shepherding: Riding with Others

ONE OF THE BEST WAYS TO EXPERIENCE MOUNTAIN BIKING IS WITH friends. I've often told my sweetheart and children, "It isn't as much about *what* you do as it is about *who* you get to do it with." The camaraderie is enjoyable, and sharing the experience with others makes it richer. I have also learned new things about the trail and about my friends when taking them up the hill for the first time. There are several keys to making this kind of experience memorable and positive.

GROUP ORGANIZATION

If there are more than two riders, it's important to place the more experienced riders at the front and the back of the group. This allows the rider in front to anticipate danger spots, difficult stretches, or rest intervals and slow down or communicate as necessary. The rider in the back can also talk to the front rider to keep the proper pace or warn of faster riders coming from behind or if a member of the group needs a break. I have unfortunately seen groups of riders or hikers strung out all over the trail with their experienced leaders in front only. It seems like groups of young men are always like this. These leaders would have no idea if one of the group members got into trouble. Large groups should not be attempted unless they have enough experienced riders to split into several more manageable cohorts.

Speed of Travel

It's critical to move at the pace of the slowest rider. It's common to pass a group of four or five riders going the opposite way. The first couple are usually well-conditioned and moving rapidly, but the last couple of riders might as well be riding alone and don't appear to be enjoying the trip. The uphill ride can be discouraging enough if left behind, but with drop-offs to your right or left most of the way, it can be even more disconcerting for a novice. In addition, the braking that is required going downhill can fatigue a novice's hands quickly (see chapter 14). If you start as a group, decide to stay together.

I remember riding down one hot summer day. I stepped to the side as two fast, experienced riders raced past going up. I then pulled back on the trail and continued downward. About a mile down the hill from where the two fast riders passed me, I came upon a young lady obviously struggling and walking her bike. It was clear she was made-up for a date, but at this point, her hair was mussed and sweat was coursing down her cheeks. She seemed distressed, so I stopped to see if everything was all right. I learned that she was with one of the speedsters and had not seen them since early in the ride. She was *not* a happy camper, and it was easy to imagine that the speedster would not get a second date. Fortunately, she was uninjured, but much worse could have happened to someone like this who was unfamiliar and unprepared for the trail. It is both irresponsible and dangerous to leave the weakest members of your group to fend for themselves. It is also selfish, and no one who does that deserves a second date.

We also work in groups to progress during this life. Family is, of course, the most important group, but we also have neighborhoods, congregations, quorums, service groups, classes, teams, troops, departments, and friendships. These groups should bring strength and support to those who are actively involved and should reach out to those who are not.

The family is the group I will focus on to illustrate the point. A family has the two most experienced members (mother and father) leading and following up on member progress during life. This becomes more difficult when one of the parents is not present or they're not on the same page.

Members of the family may move at different speeds at different times in their lives. It's also true that during the teenage or adult years, they may chafe under the concept of parental shepherding. Youth, trials, personal faith, ignorance, and transgression can all affect family members along the way. These are the times they need their experienced leaders most, and so often, this is when they're left without the help that Heavenly Father placed there for this very purpose. As parents, we cannot allow self-indulgence, distraction, fear of reaction, lack of faith, or misplaced priorities to prevent us from fulfilling those responsibilities we understood and agreed to before coming into this life. As younger members of the group or family, we should not distance ourselves to gain "independence" to the point that we lose access to this valuable guidance at a time when we need it most.

Engaged Leadership and the Prison

I recall a pleasant social visit with one of our neighbors. They had not developed any personal or organized religious values or patterns. The conversation turned to spiritual matters, and it became clear that they were concerned about their ten-year-old daughter who was beginning to show signs of being an at-risk youth through her push toward independence and desire to dress like, act like, and hang out with kids, including boys, who were several years older.

We talked about gospel values and involvement in Church organizations where she would be exposed to such teachings and broaden her circle of support. They had been attempting to teach their daughter some values but had little in their own background to aid them in the process. They were interested but later decided to opt out because it took too much time away from their own pursuits and interests to provide real parenting for their daughter.

Their excuse was that they were going to wait until she was sixteen and then let her choose for herself. This is a strategy of abdication.

What a tragedy. They may look back one day and discover that their opportunities to influence her in righteous paths occurred well before she turned sixteen. Without ongoing consistent influence, she would be unlikely to develop the foundation upon which to make wise choices in high school. This selfish parental choice could not only curse the parents' and daughter's lives for many years but also perhaps divert descendants onto strange paths. Yes, parents can make decisions that can run through families, for good or bad, for generations.

My wife and I currently serve as missionaries in a branch in the state prison near where we live. It's one of those callings/missions we had never imagined. We originally had many misunderstandings about what might go on and whether it would be dangerous. We serve in a branch covering one of the sections of buildings. Our branch includes the older geriatric men, most of whom are incarcerated for life, as well as the mental health units for men and women. An entire book could be written on what we've learned over the past two years, but there's one principle that is pertinent for this book's audience: Almost all those we serve have had long-standing and serious addictions. We lead the addiction recovery meetings that meet regularly for the men and for the mental health women. We also conduct worship services for the mental health women weekly. In every single case we are familiar with, these individuals who are now working diligently to recover from their addictions began this destructive path in elementary or junior high school. By high school, they were already engaged in seriously addictive behavior.

The addictions we deal with in these group meetings include drugs, alcohol, pornography, eating disorders, and immorality. But the real addictions and disorders beneath these are more insidious, including pride, anger, hate, self-hate, anxiety, and severe mental illness of all kinds. Yet those who have found Christ are working with all their heart, mind, and might to become something different than the person who first came to prison, and through extraordinary miracles, many are succeeding. The incredible part of this is that they're not daunted by the fact that many of them will most likely die in prison, for they look forward in hope to a better day.

CHAPTER 10: SHEPHERDING: RIDING WITH OTHERS

OPPOSING THE ROOT OF ALL TRANSGRESSIONS

A great man, and one of my mentors, once told me that selfishness was at the root of all transgressions. I have pondered that for many years and concluded that such a statement is hard to refute. In the Gospel of Matthew, the Savior is asked by a clever lawyer, in an attempt to lure him into a controversial stand, which of all the commandments was the greatest (see Matthew 22:35–40). His response confounded those who desired to trap him: "Thou shalt love the Lord thy God with all thy heart, and with all thy soul, and with all thy mind. This is the first and great commandment. And the second is like unto it, thou shalt love thy neighbour as thyself. On these two commandments hang all the law and the prophets" (Matthew 22:37–40).

If there are two great commandments, then it logically follows that there must be two great sins. The first would be putting something else before God, also known as idolatry. The second then must be like unto it, and that would be to love thyself to the exclusion of others, which sounds like selfishness to me. In fact, idolatry is in effect putting your own vain desires before God, which could also be seen as a form of selfishness. It follows then that the great sins become idolatry and selfishness, which may be combined into one great sin of selfishness. These cannot be attained without a strongly developed sinful, prideful nature known as hubris. To finish the parallel then, we would conclude that upon these great sins hang all other sins and transgressions.

I recall an example of this on the trail and how it has now turned around. I remember thirty years ago, on a trip to Sun Valley, Idaho, I had my first exposure to serious mountain biking. My sister and her husband invited us to join some friends on what I now know is one of the most challenging mountain biking loops in Sun Valley, the Adams Gulch Loop Trail. It's a seven-mile loop involving a 1,100-foot climb, which requires another five miles each way from the resort to the trailhead and back. We took our oldest son, Travis, with us, who at the time was about eleven. He has always been a superb natural athlete, but this was a long, steep ride.

We rode a few miles from the resort and up a canyon to the north of the Warm Springs side of Baldy Mountain. The trail up the canyon was enjoyable, and we crossed the stream several times, which is always fun. We then turned and began a serious climb up steep switchbacks. About a third of the way up the steepest portion, my son was unable to ride any farther. He pushed his bike around another bend, and then it became clear he really needed assistance. I put his bike on my shoulder and carried it while pushing my own bike in front of me. It was slow going, but we made it up that steep portion. By then, he was refreshed and able to continue the rest of the ride, which from that point was very technical but also mostly downhill.

The view from the trail summit was spectacular, and it was such a blessing to share that view with him. The bonus was that by me helping him along the way, his attitude stayed positive so he was able to fully appreciate the beautiful views that came later. We have since ridden many trails in those mountains together, as well as in Utah, and now he must slow down to make sure he doesn't leave *me* behind. He has become a wise trail guide himself and would not hesitate to carry my bike one day if the need arose.

The message is that sometimes it's not enough just to lead; there are times we must help shoulder the burdens of those in our flock, for they are too great for them to bear alone. This is also true in letting God lead our own efforts; there are times we must turn to Him for help in bearing our own burdens. He is always there and will respond. He created an organization because He knows we can't make it alone. Answers to prayers are often provided by real people in such organizations who hear Him and respond through ministering to each other.

Parenthood requires selfless sacrifices of time, talents, and resources to bring children to the point of partaking of the fruit of God's love (see Proverbs 11:30; Matthew 7:16–20). As a parent, I cannot read the Savior's words regarding children without experiencing tender emotions: "Then were there brought unto him little children, that he should put his hands on them, and pray: and the disciples rebuked them. But Jesus said, Suffer little children, and forbid them not, to come unto me: for of such is the kingdom of heaven" (Matthew 19:13–14). Mark and Luke include an additional statement by the Savior: "Whosoever shall not receive the kingdom of God as a little child shall in no wise enter therein" (Luke 18:17).

CHAPTER 10: SHEPHERDING: RIDING WITH OTHERS

Can you imagine, as a parent, bringing one of your children to meet the Savior, hoping for the opportunity and the impact it would surely have on their life? But you face opposition from those who think they are protecting the Savior. Then, as they're called forward, tears of gratitude water your eyes, and as they're blessed, you fall to your knees in wonder. You look at these innocent children as you absorb the lesson that we must become like them. You quietly commit yourself to do all you can to preserve their virtue and build in them a righteous purpose. What would they talk about on the way home and later at pivotal moments in their lives? Would this steel your spirit and your determination to do all you can?

This appreciation brings heartfelt understanding when reading Lehi's plea to his wayward sons: "O that ye would awake; awake from a deep sleep, yea, even from the sleep of hell, and shake off the awful chains by which ye are bound, which are the chains which bind the children of men, that they are carried away captive down to the eternal gulf of misery and woe. Awake! And arise from the dust, and hear the words of a trembling parent . . . I desire that ye should remember to observe the statutes and the judgments of the Lord" (2 Nephi 1:13–14, 16). Lehi talked about his concern because of the hard hearts of his sons Laman and Lemuel, his fear for them, and how it had weighed him down with sorrow. He promised them that they would prosper in the land if they kept the commandments, put on the armor of righteousness, and rebelled no more. This good father continued to do all he could to keep the stragglers from falling behind. His efforts continued up to his last day on the trail.

OUR ROLE AS SHEPHERDS

This too is our charge; we are to do all we can with those for whom we are shepherds. They know our voice, and most will choose to follow. Sometimes circumstances, infirmity, choices by members of our flock, or the skillful enticing of others in whom they may have mistakenly placed their trust lead them onto strange paths where we can follow only with great difficulty. There are even those occasions when contact is severed for a time. But regardless of physical, emotional, or spiritual distance, we must continue to seek after our sheep.

Then, upon the return of the prodigals, we encircle them in the arms of our love, allow them to feel God's love, and help them move forward. This is exercising the pure love of Christ, the love He has for us, called charity by Paul. It doesn't keep score, and it's willing to suffer for a long time. It is kind, it does not envy, it is not prideful, it is meek and lowly in heart, it is not selfish, it is patient and not easily provoked, it gives the benefit of the doubt and doesn't dwell on the negative, it rejoices in truth and righteousness, and it believes and hopes for all things (see 1 Corinthians 13:1–8, 13; Moroni 7:44–46).

Because of this, charity can endure all things and never fails. This requires effort to develop, of course. Mormon counseled his son to "pray unto the Father with all the energy of heart, that ye may be filled with this love . . . that when he shall appear we shall be like him" (Moroni 7:48). John further reminds us to appreciate the love our Heavenly Father has shown us as he says, "Behold, what manner of love the Father hath bestowed upon us, that we should be called the sons of God. . . . Beloved, now are we the sons of God, and it doth not yet appear what we shall be: but we know that, when he [the Savior] shall appear, we shall be like him; for we shall see him as he is. And every man that hath this hope in him purifieth himself, even as he [the Savior] is pure" (1 John 3:1–3).

This is not to imply we must become perfect. It is in the striving toward the goal that we make ourselves worthy, and the Atonement of Christ fills in the gaps. Someone once said, "Perfection is not righteousness." We attain righteousness a little at a time by setting a pattern that includes loving God with all our hearts and loving others as ourselves. This pattern is a covenant path bordered by following Christ's commandments the best we can and serving others along the way.

Do all you can to keep your group together, and do not become distracted by vain pursuits or wounded pride or give your heart over to selfishness, dark thoughts, or anger. These are the opposite of the love of which John and the Savior spoke. The Savior Himself tells us still today, "Come unto me, all ye that labour and are heavy laden, and I will give you rest" (Matthew 11:28). As we do this, we're promised that the Savior's yoke is easy and His burden is light and that we will be strengthened to bear the burdens that are placed upon us (see

CHAPTER 10: SHEPHERDING: RIDING WITH OTHERS

Matthew 11:29–30; Mosiah 24:15). In so doing, and with time, you will bring your flock safely home, and great will be your joy with them (see John 4:35–37; Doctrine and Covenants 18:14–16).

11
Knowing Your Personal Limits

KNOWING OUR LIMITATIONS IS ALWAYS IMPORTANT. HOWEVER, THIS is particularly important on the Mueller Park Trail during three specific time periods. The first time is the early spring riding period. The weather is unpredictable, and careful preparation is important. But the more important factor is that most of us do not maintain our conditioning at as high a level during the winter as we do at other times of the year. It's possible for the heartiest of riders to move to road biking and ride during the Utah winters or to have a regular aerobic indoor alternative; however, human nature and the cold weather make this difficult to maintain.

Northern Utah is a wonderful place to live if you want to have a legitimate winter but you don't want to have too much. The Wasatch Front typically will have about eight to ten weeks of what I consider frigid weather (thirty degrees and below). Interspersed there will be several weeks of "Indian summer" where the temperatures can rise to the forty- to fifty-degree range. This really isn't too bad, as winter goes, and allows for reasonably pleasant road riding if you dress properly.

The trail to Big Rock is usually mostly clear of snow by late April, so mountain biking can resume. When resuming regular rides in the spring, it's important to understand that you will be working at a slower pace than you were toward the end of the previous riding season when your conditioning was at a peak. To avoid early setbacks like pulled muscles, it's best to work gradually back up to an adequate level of conditioning.

Second, riding at the end of the fall has many of the same weather-related issues as does early season riding. These again have to do with dressing properly and particularly protecting your fingers, ears, and face, as has been discussed previously. Spring and fall riding can also involve slogging through soft or muddy ground, which takes more energy and slows your overall rate of travel. This also can require careful management of your energy usage and water intake during a ride.

The third situation where you must know your limits is perhaps the least obvious when you're riding—it's the mid-summer period when high temperatures can wear you down. On a hot day, it's best to ride early before the temperature rises, but that's not always convenient. As a result, the trail can have rather heavy usage during the warmer morning hours and then again in the later afternoon when the angle of the sun is better but the ground still radiates heat. If you choose to ride the trail during a warmer period, be sure to hydrate before you begin and continue to take liquids during your ride.

There have been times when I have not hydrated sufficiently or I find it to be warmer than anticipated. The heat doesn't bring a rider down all at once—it's a subtle attack. You may notice that your bike seems just a little bit squirrelly, or you're weaving a tiny bit and your balance is slightly off. There can be a dizzy, lightheaded feeling as if you had hyperventilated. Should you notice these symptoms, it's a good idea to find a shady cooler spot (usually on an inside bend or near a stream by one of the bridges), cool down, and hydrate. After a rest and some water, it might be wise to consider turning around and riding down. You are close to your personal limit for that day.

I will add one more special case. I have occasionally taken a friend from out of town up the trail. If the individual has come from a low elevation, one of the coasts for example, it's important to use additional discretion due to the change in altitude and their inability to properly acclimate. The result for the careless soul is a case of early-stage burnout and the need for a long afternoon nap. Any type of exhaustion,

Spiritual Vertigo

Life also can sneak up on us sometimes, and we find ourselves spiritually disoriented and out of balance. The principle I will emphasize here is one taught to me by one of my most influential religious leaders, my mission president, Allen C. Rozsa, on the occasion of my exit interview at the end of my mission in 1977. The perspective gained has been critical in managing through several periods of my life when spiritual threats were subtle but nonetheless real.

He taught me about the principle of "spiritual vertigo." Before explaining the principle, some background is necessary. Allen Rozsa came straight to the mission field after a career as an Air Force pilot. He flew during World War II, the Korean War, and the Vietnam War. He had flown a wide variety of aircraft, resulting in many inspirational stories, and we loved to get him on the subject during our meetings. He was one of my personal heroes. I loved him and his wife with all my heart. They are the two people who have been, and remain today, most influential in my younger life. They welcomed me as part of their family, and I still feel that to this day. On this occasion, he counseled me in preparation for my return home from full-time service. I had completely immersed myself in the work and believe now that he recognized that those who had done so needed a little extra preparation for effective transition to the next stage of their life.

He counseled me to beware of spiritual vertigo. He explained that one of the greatest dangers in flying was losing perspective regarding where you are in space and not relying on your instruments to help you get back on track. He asked me to think of taking off in a jet airliner. The acceleration and lift as the jet climbs is obvious. Then the rate of ascent decreases as the aircraft approaches its cruising altitude. The occupants experience the feeling of acceleration at take-off and the steep climb and can mistake the decrease in the rate of ascent for descending. In fact, the aircraft is still gaining altitude but at a lower rate, and the human senses are deceived into feeling the aircraft is losing altitude. He explained how dangerous this can be for a pilot at night or in clouds when there are no visible points of reference.

He then related this to my situation. He warned me that I had been immersed in something so completely and had been growing spiritually on such a steep curve that when I returned to home, school, and regular life, I could develop a feeling that I was losing my spiritual connection when, in fact, I was continuing to grow but at a lower rate. He went on to explain that new converts following their baptism also can go through a period when they struggle spiritually. An early opportunity to serve, continuing instruction, and study can be helpful in these situations.

Over the years, as well as for this book, I have discussed this subject with those who have recently returned from similar service, some who had completed their assignments as religious leaders as well as a variety of others who had completed less visible assignments (but ones that took everything they had to effectively perform). I have also interviewed those who had gone through family breakups and other personal or financial crises. I found no exceptions. All described, without realizing, a sense of spiritual vertigo that at the time added to their perceived burdens, and only in retrospect did they see it more clearly.

I remember one returned mission president telling me that the eighteen months immediately following the completion of his full-time service was one of the toughest transitions of his life.

Sometimes such periods can occur as a result of one of the great trials of our lives. The loss of a close family member on whom you have depended, serious illness or injury, financial upheaval, or a disruption in the family unit like divorce can bring about vertigo or even a period of free fall.

Those who experience spiritual vertigo know well the feeling of steep spiritual growth and sense a change. It can be frustrating, almost like hearing an amputee talk about still being able to feel their missing appendage and having an itch that cannot be scratched. These intensely spiritual experiences are foundational in your life. Those who gave all their heart, might, mind, and soul (see 2 Nephi 25:29), exceeded expectations, and finished with honor, knowledge, and faith, as Paul advised (see 1 Corinthians 9:24), should not be surprised that their growth might level off a bit.

It then becomes their responsibility to recognize that growth is continuing. It continues in part by overcoming the very challenges and confusion faced during such transitions. The task then is to re-apply the developed strength and talents to the new situation. Your faithfulness and service has established a pattern that you can reassert.

Starting with God from Where We Are

We must all start from where we are rather than where we are supposed to be or where others expect us to be. Reasserting our established pattern allows us to again feel growth as we stay focused on the daily, weekly, and monthly religious practices that keep us close to the Lord. You may return to activities that feel far removed from those you were accustomed to. But you will find your footing in the next phase of your life, unless you intentionally throw it all to the wind. It's reassuring to know that God knows exactly where we are and is always willing to start from there.

It is those who become distracted by the things of the world that misjudge their situation and are most susceptible to discouragement. It isn't very different from moving to a new job or city, or being released from a responsibility you love. We sometimes find that the new situation requires us to make new friends or adjust to new working or social conditions. Perhaps acceptance is slow in coming, or the overall circumstances are not as favorable as those in your previous location. Sometimes we feel anxiety or awkwardness as we begin anew. This is the time to check your conditioning, spiritually hydrate, adjust your view of how to effectively apply your spiritual strengths, and move forward.

It's not the time to look back and dwell on how good things were in the past or search for excuses. Of course, our past matters a lot. It forms our base of experience, and it's something we can learn from. However, dwelling on the past is not a successful strategy. We are where we are today, and God is more interested in who we are becoming rather than who we were. It's time to gather and refresh yourself with the Spirit and press forward, remaining steadfast and making choices that will define who we become.

The Savior Himself warned us of this danger when he said to those who desired to follow Him but were distracted by other things, "No man, having put his hand to the plough, and looking back, is fit for the kingdom of God" (Luke 9:62). Job's example and words after losing everything provide inspiration about faithful endurance. "Naked came I out of my mother's womb, and naked shall I return thither: the Lord gave, and the Lord hath taken away; blessed be the name of the Lord. . . . For I know that my redeemer liveth, and that he shall stand at the latter day upon the earth: And though after my skin worms destroy this body, yet in my flesh shall I see God. . . . I made a covenant. . . . Let me be weighed in an even balance, that God may know mine integrity" (Job 1:21; 19:25–26; 31:1, 6).

Nephi gave us wise counsel on this subject during his great discourse on baptism and endurance:

> And now . . . after ye have gotten into this strait and narrow path, I would ask if all is done? Behold, I say unto you, Nay; for ye have not come thus far save it were by the word of Christ with unshaken faith in him, relying wholly upon the merits of him who is mighty to save.
>
> Wherefore, ye must press forward with a steadfastness in Christ, having a perfect brightness of hope, and a love of God and of all men. Wherefore, if ye shall press forward, feasting upon the word of Christ, and endure to the end, behold, thus saith the Father: Ye shall have eternal life. . . .
>
> This is the way; and there is no other way. . . . This is the doctrine of Christ, and . . . of the Father, and of the . . . Holy Ghost. (2 Nephi 31:19–21)

The way to avoid the downward pull of spiritual vertigo and the world is to press forward with steadfastness, seek out those who share your conviction, share each other's burdens, and then make sure you continue to stand on "good ground." By doing this, we cannot be dragged down. The counsel to us is clear: "Wherefore, stand ye in holy places, and be not moved" (Doctrine and Covenants 87:8).

12

Respecting the Trail

RIDING IN THE MOUNTAINS AT 5,000 TO 7,000 FEET CAN BE A BEAU-tiful experience. The combination of breathtaking views, smells that awaken the senses, and healthy exertion is hard to beat. The single track offers all of these and more. Respecting this beautiful environment is the foundation of preserving it for future experiences and generations. However, wherever we go, it seems there are those who are polluters; they seem to have little concern for anything other than themselves and their own gratification. They use, abuse, and walk away, seemingly unconcerned about how they might have left the area for the next person or how they impact others who might be there at the same time.

On the trail, there are a few who simply drop what they no longer need and move on. This can include litter of all types, dog or horse feces, and clothing. There are also those who deface the trail, which includes building the occasional illegal campfire in the center of the trail, defacing trees, or riding out of control and repeatedly skidding their tires, making deep furrows on the trail that are eroded by the rain.

Tire skidding is most damaging when the edge of the trail is torn apart, allowing erosion to eat into the trail itself. This, of course, is wholly avoidable by maintaining responsible speeds, communicating ahead, and understanding how to utilize both brakes and their individual touch to avoid unnecessary damage to the trail. The litter aspect is also avoidable by simply caring a bit more and accepting some responsibility for your actions. While most of these activities seem like little things and must continue unabated over time to cause serious or permanent damage, there are a few that can be devastating.

Setting a campfire in an illegal or careless location with thick foliage and overhanging trees is one of these. I have ridden in two different areas in Idaho after the ravages of a forest fire. The trail is still there, of course, but the countryside will likely not be the same again during my lifetime. It's tragic, but once done, some damage cannot be easily undone.

Our lives are in many ways similar to a beautiful mountain path. There is wear and tear that occurs with responsible usage, and there's natural erosion that's unavoidable and comes as the years run by. However, there are also ways one can produce unnecessary or premature damage. I suggest that there are three basic ways to erode or pollute a life. I will describe them as "physical," "spiritual," and "prospects" erosion.

Physical and Spiritual Erosion

Physical and spiritual erosion are connected. It doesn't matter which one leads—the other one soon follows. A person simply can't fill their mind with anger, wickedness, lust, and perversion without it changing their behavior, dress, and countenance. Likewise, a person can't damage and pollute their own physical body without it changing their attentiveness toward spiritual nourishment and dampening or destroying faith.

Paul asked the Corinthians, "Know ye not that your body is the temple of the Holy Ghost?" (1 Corinthians 6:19) and "Know ye not that ye are the temple of God, and that the Spirit of God dwelleth in you? If any man defile the temple of God, him shall God destroy; for the temple of God is holy, which temple ye are" (1 Corinthians 3:16–17). Alma likewise reminded us that the Holy Ghost "doth not dwell in unholy temples" (Alma 7:21). John reminded us that the

CHAPTER 12: RESPECTING THE TRAIL

Holy Ghost's ability to dwell with us is dependent on our obedience (see 1 John 3:24). Paul put it all together most eloquently when he taught, "And what agreement hath the temple of God with idols? for ye are the temple of the living God; as God hath said, I will dwell in them, and walk in them; and I will be their God, and they shall be my people. Wherefore come out from among them, and be ye separate, saith the Lord, and touch not the unclean thing; and I will receive you" (2 Corinthians 6:16–17). It's such a fitting analogy to be used by the prophets because of the historic reverence God's people had toward temples and the importance they played in their lives. What better way to illustrate the holiness of one's own body, which was created by God Himself?

Our society today seems to have completely disregarded the concept that our bodies are sacred temples of God and the Holy Spirit. The concept that our physical body is a gift and was intentionally created in the image of God (see Genesis 1:26–27; 9:6) is generally ignored in favor of the justification that "It's my body, and I can do what I want with it." As a result, our physical bodies in many cases are polluted, abused, mutilated, and more likely to be used as billboards or pin cushions than as temples. Would you deface a sacred building with graffiti or punch random holes in the walls for what, in your opinion, should be decorative doors or windows?

The scriptures compare the human body to the most holy of Old Testament and modern structures, the holy temple where God dwells. Both Moses and Solomon were given specific directions regarding the construction and use of the tabernacle and temple. They were to use their finest treasures, not because God needed the wealth but because it helped set these sacred places apart in the minds of the people. It did not belong to them; it belonged to God. It was not to be used as a blank canvas upon which they could put any decoration desired. While such activities related to defacing or mutilating our bodies with tattoos, intentional scarring, gratuitous operations, or multiple piercings do pose some serious potential physical, emotional, and mental health problems,[27] they are more symptomatic of a lack of respect for

27. Liesa Goins, "Tattoos: Are They Safe?," WebMD, Feb. 11, 2011, https://www.webmd.com/skin-problems-and-treatments/features/tattoos-are-they-safe.

our temple and God Himself since it was His gift to us. Unfortunately, such outward bodily disrespect is often associated with inward disrespect and pollution.

I can't help but think about the twisted joy that must come to Satan when he is successful in convincing humans that their bodies are meaningless or without value, especially since he forfeited such a gift. Can he actually get men to live a life that denies any advantage that comes with having a body? That one is hard to answer, but I can imagine that such a thought would give the adversary great pleasure.

PROTECTING OUR TEMPLES

There is no serious difference of opinion regarding the damage, premature aging, and causes of death from internal bodily abuse due to alcohol, tobacco, and drug usage. Statistics for causes of death in 2006 indicated that the top five causes were, in order, heart attacks, cancer, stroke, chronic lower respiratory (lung disease), and unintentional accidents (primarily vehicle-related). Virtually every year since then, it has been the same. These five causes accounted for two-thirds of all recorded deaths in 2006. The leading cause of death for those under the age of thirty-four remained historically consistent as unintentional accidents.[28] Which one of these causes is not heavily associated with the use or abuse of the referenced substances? None—they are the primary contributors to all these causes. To illustrate the point more effectively, let's take just one of these health threats and its indirect effect on others: smoking. In 2006, the surgeon general issued a detailed report on the health consequences of involuntary exposure to tobacco smoke (referred to as secondhand smoke). The conclusions were clear:

1. There is no risk-free level of exposure to secondhand smoke.
2. Secondhand smoke causes lung cancer.
3. Secondhand smoke causes heart disease.
4. Secondhand smoke causes acute respiratory effects.

---

28. Melonie Heron, Donna L. Hoyert, Shery L. Murphy, Jiaquan Xu, Kenneth D. Kochanek, and Betzaida Tejada-Vera, "Deaths: Final Data for 2006," *National Vital Statistics Report* 57, no. 14 (Apr. 2006), http://www.cdc.gov/nchs/data/nvsr/nvsr57/nvsr57_14.pdf.

5. Secondhand smoke can cause sudden infant death syndrome (SIDS) and other health consequences in infants and children.

6. Separating smokers from nonsmokers, cleaning the air, and ventilating buildings cannot eliminate secondhand smoke exposure.[29]

A further study published in April 2010 concluded that a combination of four "unhealthy behaviors—smoking, lack of exercise, poor diet, and substantial alcohol consumption—increases the risk of premature death . . . [by] 12 years"[30]

When we abuse our bodies, we not only lower our self-image, remove our access to the Holy Ghost, and distance ourselves from God, but we also destroy ourselves as well as damage countless others around us (see chapter 2).

President Boyd K. Packer has said:

My patriarchal blessing counseled: "Guard and protect [your body]—take nothing into it that shall harm the organs thereof because it is sacred. It is the instrument of your mind and the foundation of your character." I found in the Word of Wisdom a principle with a promise. The principle: Care for your body; avoid habit-forming stimulants, tea, coffee, tobacco, liquor, and drugs. Such addictive things do little more than relieve a craving which they caused in the first place.[31]

He further stated regarding our outward appearance, "You would not paint a temple with dark pictures or symbols or graffiti or even initials. Do not do so with your body."[32]

President Gordon B. Hinckley has counseled parents on the rearing of young people that we must do the following:

---

29. Office on Smoking and Health, *The Health Consequences of Involuntary Exposure to Tobacco Smoke: A Report of the Surgeon General* (U.S. Department of Health and Human Services, 2006), https://www.ncbi.nlm.nih.gov/books/NBK44324/.

30. Office on Smoking and Health, *The Health Consequences.*

31. Boyd K. Packer, "Ye Are the Temple of God," *Ensign,* Nov. 2000, 72.

32. Boyd K. Packer, "Ye Are the Temple of God," 73.

Teach them to respect their bodies. The practice is growing among young people of tattooing and piercing their bodies. The time will come when they will regret it, but it will then be too late. . . .

What do they hope to gain by this painful process? Is there "anything virtuous, lovely, or of good report or praiseworthy" (Articles of Faith 1:13) in having unseemly so-called art impregnated into the skin to be carried throughout life, all the way down to old age and death? They must be counseled to shun it. They must be warned to avoid it. . . .

I submit that it is an uncomely thing, and yet a common thing, to see young men with ears pierced for earrings, not for one pair only, but for several.

They have no respect for their appearance. Do they think it clever or attractive to so adorn themselves?

I submit it is not adornment. It is making ugly that which was attractive. Not only are ears pierced, but other parts of the body as well, even the tongue. It is absurd. . . .

Teach your sons and daughters to avoid illegal drugs as they would the plague. The use of these narcotics will destroy them. They cannot so abuse their bodies; they cannot so build within themselves vicious and enslaving appetites without doing incalculable injury. One habit calls for another, until the victim in so many cases is led down to a situation of utter helplessness, with loss of all self-control and habituated to a point where it cannot be broken.[33]

The warning is clear: We cannot engage in defacing our personal temple internally or externally, spiritually or emotionally, and have it remain a temple in which the Holy Spirit can dwell. Some of these activities erode and pollute over time, while others can lead to rapid destruction, including spiritual and physical death.

Erosion of Prospects

Erosion of prospects is a follow-up event resulting from the first two types of pollution. I have seen some high mountain trails that have lost their edge, and without attention, whole sections of the trail have eroded away, preventing future usage or making it extremely

---

33. Gordon B. Hinckley, "Your Greatest Challenge, Mother," *Ensign*, Nov. 2000, 99.

CHAPTER 12: RESPECTING THE TRAIL

hazardous. Our futures can be marred or severely limited because of engaging in foolish behaviors without consideration for unintended possible outcomes. Imagine how your future job prospects might be affected by a felony conviction on your record or as a result of moderate brain damage or other physically limiting damage or paralysis. Some of the most common long-term impacts of these kinds of behavior that we see in our current calling to minister at the prison are teeth that have completely rotted out due to drug or alcohol use to the point they cannot be repaired and must be pulled and replaced by complete dentures even at a young age (thirties and forties). We also see severe mental illness and physical damage, including severe anxiety, dementia, paranoia, schizophrenia, and depression.

It matters little if the permanent change in our prospects was unintended. Certainly, too many have bought into the adversary's campaign that we can do anything now and the effects are far off, temporary, or maybe even minimal, so why not? The hard truth is that the enjoyment and satisfaction of life do not stop when you are thirty-something, and those who disregard their bodies risk the loss of much true joy along the way and valuable time at the end when their journey is unnecessarily cut short.

Also consider a shortsighted view toward education, particularly the K–12 grades, and how it might leave you wholly unprepared for the buffetings of the world. I spoke to a young man recently who attended a local high school. He, already at a young age, bore the scars of the internal and external neglect and abuse of his temple. He was a junior at the time and had decided not to make a serious effort at school.

His attendance and tardiness were chronic and his grades dismal, resulting in exclusion from participation in competitive sports, something he was once very accomplished in. His behavior was increasingly rebellious and selfish, and his attitude became more negative each time I saw him. He had completely lost the light I once saw in his eyes, and his desire to achieve was gone. His response was that he already had an opportunity to earn decent money as soon as he graduated (at a menial job) and that good grades and further education were therefore unimportant. I felt this was a far-reaching decision for a sixteen-year-old to be making and that he couldn't possibly have made it with a clear view of its possible outcomes.

I attempted to speak to him about his choices, but he was unwilling to consider a different point of view. The poor young man put himself in a position where his options would be severely limited should his specific plan not work out. He, of course, was unwilling to consider what it might be like for the next forty years in such a work environment because he just wanted to be done with school. Yes, perspective can change, and I pray that it does. But how many lost years and opportunities will it take before he figures it out and starts over? How many doors of opportunity that he doesn't even know exist will be permanently closed before he figures out the unintended consequences of his unwise decisions?

Another type of prospect erosion is time on this earth. I loved my father dearly and would like nothing better than to have lunch with him today and discuss my writing and obtain his guidance. He was a wonderful and hardworking man. He was also an honest and honorable man but was not particularly religious until late in his life. While he made some courageous and righteous decisions in the last ten years of his life, it was cut short by decisions he made during his teens through his forties.

During his younger years, he developed serious alcohol and smoking habits. He overcame both during his late forties because it was becoming life- and job-threatening, but the internal damage was already done. He passed away at the age of sixty-eight from complications with his lungs and cancer. The hidden curse in such behavior is that it not only takes you prematurely, but it also limits and then destroys your life along the way. He was in and out of hospitals his last ten years, and from his forties on, he was severely limited and literally could not engage in any mildly strenuous activity without gasping for air. That's right—he could not "run and not be weary, and shall walk and not faint" (Doctrine and Covenants 89:20).

He did much good during his life in all phases of his involvement, but he was robbed of much that he might have enjoyed, and we lost some of our precious association with him because of unwise choices that destroyed his earthly temple. He also missed important opportunities to grow spiritually and find true joy because of his long spiritual

There Is Always Hope on the True Path

Satan has an endless bag of ideas and toys to pull young people down a long path. More recent subjects that are only now beginning to produce dangerous results include vaping, gender reassignment therapies and surgeries, legalization of all manner of drugs, and the introduction of mushrooms and pot into items that look like candy. We can be sure an endless variety of things will continue to pop us that, by the time we understand their danger, will have destroyed an entire generation as did smoking and alcohol.

There are many wonderful promises in the scriptures for those who respect the trail and their earthly temples. "They that wait upon the Lord shall renew their strength; they shall mount up with wings as eagles; they shall run, and not be weary; and they shall walk, and not faint" (Isaiah 40:31). Now, *that* sounds like someone in good health. We are further promised, "And all saints who remember to keep and do these sayings, walking in obedience to the commandments, shall receive health in their navel and marrow to their bones; And shall find wisdom and great treasures of knowledge, even hidden treasures; And shall run and not be weary, and shall walk and not faint. And I, the Lord, give unto them a promise, that the destroying angel shall pass by them, as the children of Israel, and not slay them" (Doctrine and Covenants 89:18–21).

Our Heavenly Father wants us to pass every test and overcome every obstacle. He gave us a spirit encased in a work of eternal fine art called a human body so that we might have success during this mortal life in preparing ourselves to return to Him. This gift is also given so that we might experience meaningful joy and happiness along the path. The counsel we have received from God and His servants, as well as personal revelatory guidance, if followed, will make that possible.

13
Picking the Right Line

THERE ARE TECHNICAL STRETCHES ALONG THE PATH THAT REQUIRE additional attention. These can be encumbered with rocks and roots or may involve slick wet hills, narrow bridges, loose gravel, or sand. Each of these requires adjustment. The most challenging are always easier if you pick a line through the stretch and predetermine how you'll avoid the most troublesome spots as well as how you'll hit the obstacles you cannot avoid.

There is a spot about 300 feet below the "pipeline" that presents such a problem. As you approach the spot coming uphill, there's a steep smooth rise of about thirty feet that culminates in a hump over a large root with a low-hanging branch. After the hump, there's a spot where the trail is split into two levels with about a foot between the levels. The lower level is good when coming down, but staying high helps keep momentum going.

Because the trail is split, each side of the path is only about six inches wide. The trail then curves sharply right (blind corner), there's a wide crown of an exposed boulder on the right side that you must roll over, and the lower part of the trail has roots that rob you of your momentum. The trail now is no longer split, and there's a 10- to 15-foot downward roll with a large root angled right to left across the trail. The top of this root is smooth from wearing, but it can be quite slick when wet and redirect your front wheel if not hopped over or hit at greater than a 45-degree angle. If your wheel is redirected, it turns toward the drop-off—not good.

After the root, you have about ten feet to pick up some momentum because there's a tree on the edge of the trail with a root system perpendicular to the trail running straight across. This requires a hop to get over the root, and the line is to the right toward the lesser thickness of the root system. Drifting to the left takes you into the trunk of the tree—also not good. As you can see, picking the proper line and sticking to it allows you to maintain momentum and overcome a succession of obstacles that come one after another. Getting off-line at any point will likely prevent you from overcoming the next obstacle. It is also clear that having some familiarity with the trail so you can anticipate this rapid succession of obstacles is helpful.

For five decades, I enjoyed snow skiing at a high level and have occasionally participated in or watched individuals run a tight slalom or downhill course. The momentum, strength, and rhythm necessary to successfully negotiate such a course are inspiring. Every competition has its moments when a skier catches an edge or gets off-line for one reason or another and misses a gate. It simply is not possible to recover from such slight deviations at unforgiving speeds.

A Covenant People

Our passage along life's path is similar in so many ways. It is best, of course, not to go off-line in the first place. However, God provided a process, called repentance, that allows us to get back on track if it becomes necessary. One of the guiding principles we follow in our home is that we do everything we can to "not make a mistake the first time." What does this mean? Well, we recognize that commandments, covenants, virtuous standards, house rules, laws of the land, and so on are created as a result of needed direction. If we do our best to honor and keep our promises to the Lord, we give ourselves the best opportunity to succeed. Setting a good example is one important reason we do this, but there's a deeper purpose. Therefore, covenant people should be grateful to Heavenly Father for our many blessings and should always attempt to stand in "holy places" (Doctrine and Covenants 87:8).

It has therefore been our family mantra that we strive to keep the commandments every time and not allow them to become "negotiations." We recognize that once we compromise on one of these covenants, commandments, or rules, it is *not* a rule, law, or a commandment to us anymore; it becomes a "negotiation." This means that once we have crossed that particular line, we stand on the other side. As long as we stand there, we are faced with repeated self-negotiation each time that particular rule or promise is tested, trying to decide how we will behave the next time.

This is a state in which no one can exist for very long. It's a slippery slope. Unchecked, it soon becomes less and less of a negotiation, then a habit, and finally an established part of our new behavior. Individuals who have succumbed usually find themselves arguing, rationalizing, or justifying their newly developed pattern. This reinforcement is what leads to hardened hearts and stiff-neckedness, as described frequently in the scriptures. Jacob taught his people the following:

> The Spirit speaketh the truth and lieth not. . . . It speaketh of things as they really are, and of things as they really will be. . . . These things are manifested unto us plainly, for the salvation of our souls. . . .
>
> But behold, the Jews were a stiffnecked people; and they despised the words of plainness . . . and sought for things that they could not understand . . . because of their blindness, which blindness came by looking beyond the mark, they must needs fall; for God hath taken away his plainness from them, and delivered unto them many things which they cannot understand, because they desired it . . . that they may stumble. (Jacob 4:13–14)

This strange path that someone may find themselves on goes nowhere, but it does provide many diversions and excuses along the way. Most individuals who have fallen into this way do not cease believing in God. Instead, they tend to mold Him into something that will fit into their new and ever-changing lifestyle, rejecting the plain and precious parts of the gospel. This process of removing God from His throne and replacing Him with themselves may work while the sun is shining and the weather calm. But when clouds gather and storms threaten, it will fail.

I have addressed this in a previous chapter. However, it may be helpful to point out a strange end point in this devolution of relationship with God and spiritual famine. Individuals overcome in this way become increasingly unclear about the purpose of this life and what happens after death. Is there a judgment? Are there kingdoms or blessings that accrue based on how we live? Usually, the justification wins out and they conclude that there's nothing worth striving for after this life or that, regardless of behavior in this life, there will be an opportunity for equality of outcomes for everyone. Occasionally, they come to a most extraordinary conclusion that they will have the opportunity to change after death when they discover their great error and will be given some kind of "fast pass" to the front of the line. A more recent twist on this with former Christians and Latter-day Saints is a pop-culture investigation of reincarnation—not as practiced in Eastern religions but the idea that if they don't get it right this time, they will have a never-ending series of rebirths to try it again. This sounds a lot like video game regeneration and may be appealing to the younger generation but, in fact, is a destructive counterfeit.

Key to Becoming

The key to remember is that we are "becoming" something during this life, and we do it by how we live and what we hold most dear. God loves us, and He also respects our choices. He will not force us to accept something or live differently after death. The Lord has stated clearly, "And they who remain shall also be quickened; nevertheless, they shall return again to their own place, to enjoy that which they are willing to receive, because they were not willing to enjoy that which they might have received. For what doth it profit a man if a gift is bestowed upon him, and he receive not the gift?" (Doctrine and Covenants 88:32–33).

The way back for a covenanting people is to repent and make a covenant or renew a covenant. This means we must take action to move back to "good ground" or a "holy place." Note that it must be *our* choice and decision. Yes, this applies to house rules as well. The

CHAPTER 13: PICKING THE RIGHT LINE

more we develop an attitude of compromising, and then negotiating on small things, the further we get out of our planned line.

In the book of Alma, Ammon and his brethren were instrumental in converting thousands of their mortal enemies, Lamanites, to Christ and the gospel. In the process of full conversion, this people made a powerful, faith-filled decision to break with their wicked past. This is often seen as one action, but a careful review of the decision indicates it was really a two-step process.

First, we see that the people of Ammon (as they were eventually called) were so committed not to go back to their former hateful ways that "they did lay down the weapons of their rebellion, that they did not fight against God any more, neither against any of their brethren" (Alma 23:7). These weapons of rebellion were clearly their former attitudes, doubt, hate, and a variety of other conflict-causing behaviors. This opened the way for them to take the next step: They "were converted unto the Lord . . . [and] laid down the weapons of their rebellion, yea, all their weapons of war" (Alma 23:13). This soul-saving decision involved a commitment never to be tempted again, as explained: "They took their swords, and all the weapons . . . and they did bury them up deep in the earth" (Alma 24:17).

We, like the Lamanite converts, should be disciplining ourselves in preparation for something. Why not make that something worthwhile? In our family, we have discovered that the key is choosing not to miss church, scripture study, family prayers, service opportunities, family activities, or opportunities to uplift others, to name but a few, the first time. We have also sadly seen the tragic results or long diversions in the lives of those we love when such guidance is ignored. Spiritual momentum is best maintained by not falling down the first time whenever possible.

THE SAVIOR'S PERSONAL GIFT TO ALL

Now, in spite of our collective and individual best efforts, we find ourselves falling down on occasion anyway. There is plenty of that in life without adding more ourselves. But the Lord said without hesitation, "I lay down my life for the sheep" (John 10:15) and "[I] suffered these things for all, that they might not suffer if they would repent"

(Doctrine and Covenants 19:16). Our Savior willingly took upon Him our sins, pains, wounds at the hand of others, and all our other burdens and asks only that we do our best to accept this great Atonement through the exercise of our faith by obedience and repentance. In doing this, we receive His grace, which brings peace, not confusion; healing, not pain; and a heart full of light rather than darkness.

It's miraculous that mastering the principle of choosing the correct line to follow and sticking with it not only gives us spiritual elevation, but the principle is also transferable when dealing with other rules and laws such as the rules of your home, staying on top of homework, and honoring the commitments you have made to your team or in the workplace. Such spiritual momentum also makes our travel along the narrow path seem easier, our burdens become lighter, and our hopes become brighter.

There's one more critical component necessary to make this a successful process. Those in our respective flocks must be able to exercise their own right to choose, as they are able, and take title to these obligations themselves. This means, in the case of our teenagers, that it's one thing for them to tell their friends that they can't engage in certain activities on Sunday, watch an inappropriate movie, or stay out past curfew because their parents won't let them. But it's entirely different when a teenage son says to his friends that he isn't going to a particular movie or Sunday sporting event because he doesn't feel good about it *himself*. This position has conviction and commands respect from his peers because he is expressing his own feelings.

Certainly, our interactions with children change as they develop perspective and maturity and begin to more clearly understand right from wrong. It seems sometimes that real parenting doesn't begin until your children become more independent. There is no magical age where this happens. But increasingly as children mature, we parent by consent and because of respect and trust rather than simply because we're parents.

My wife and I have realized that when we place our teenagers or young adults in the position that makes them the most responsible—that of exercising their own freedom to choose—it can be quite uncomfortable for them. When faced with a particular teenage dilemma, we have tried to make it clear to them what the Lord's position

CHAPTER 13: PICKING THE RIGHT LINE

is on the particular matter and also clearly describe what our position is on that same matter and what choices therefore would constitute choosing the right course. Then we pull the "responsibility trigger" (you know, the one that makes a teenager groan).

We point out that they understand the Lord's will and their parents' will, so they are now free to choose for themselves. One of our sons confessed as a teenager that he would much rather have had us tell him what to do. Our responsibility as parents is to make sure they have a clear understanding of what is right and why and that we trust them to make a wise decision. When it works, they are more likely to take ownership of the decision. When they choose unwisely, we still love them and try to help them understand that they are neither forsaken by us nor God. They will often claim that we simply don't understand why they want to stray along an unwise path, but the truth is that we do understand enough to know that we don't agree. Disagreement is not ignorance.

This leaves one unaddressed issue, which is dealt with by examining one aspect of our spiritual gifts. Paul describes several of the gifts of the Spirit (see 1 Corinthians 12:3–11; Hebrews 2:4). One particular gift mentioned is "differences of administration" (1 Corinthians 12:5). Latter-day revelation confirms this as a gift of the Spirit as the Lord states, "To some it is given by the Holy Ghost to know the differences of administration, as it will be pleasing unto the same Lord, according as the Lord will . . . according to the conditions of the children of men" (Doctrine and Covenants 46:15). This clearly applies to how each of us may approach our opportunities and obligations to serve God in accordance with His will. It also applies to how we manage, with Him, our individual lives. This clearly applies to magnifying church callings in accordance with the Lord's will.

DIFFERENCES OF ADMINISTRATION

Knowing that differences of administration is a gift helps us recognize differing applications—as we learn and grow in managing our personal life, then our life with our spouse, then our life with children and all the associated complexities—and helps us balance and properly prioritize along the way. This gift, like many of the others, can be received more abundantly ("according to His will") as one grows in faithful experience (see Doctrine and Covenants 46:15; Hebrews 2:4).

One of my nephews had completed a very successful and honorable two-year mission and was struggling with spiritual vertigo and readjustment. Neither of his parents had served in that way, and they came to me asking for input on how they could respond to his repeated comment that they didn't know what he was going through. I agreed to write him a letter because he could not make that particular argument in response to my counsel. I felt the Lord's inspiration in the response as I explained that while he had just completed an important foundational experience in his life, such an experience was insufficient to teach him all that would be necessary in this next important stage to manage the increasing complexity of life and continue to make progress.

I counseled him that his bishop and parents were his best resource because they have rich experience in this type of administration. In this case, this extraordinary young man simply didn't know how to manage school, athletics, and the impending idea of marriage. Of course, he was on a steep learning curve, but Heavenly Father had surrounded him with wise and experienced stewards. Seeking and heeding their counsel, along with praying and staying faithful, helped him organize himself and prepare every needful thing (see Doctrine and Covenants 88:119–120).

Like my nephew, we all learn, as we actively and seriously include the Lord in our travel along the path, that with time and necessity, the windows of heaven open wider so that we might receive more abundantly the gifts of the Spirit and increased knowledge. Until then, we are wise in learning from those who already have such gifts. We are told that as we seek earnestly, always remember for what these gifts are given, keep the commandments, and ask according to the will of God, it will be done even as we ask (see Matthew 7:7; 1 Corinthians 14:12; Doctrine and Covenants 46:8–9, 30).

It is therefore good to plan a line of progress, but it is better if we use the Lord's planned line and follow it under the guidance of the Holy Ghost. We learn the Lord's plan by developing a pattern of behavior that includes study and prayer as well as learning from those the Lord has placed among us as our personal shepherds.

14

The Downhill Ride

My typical morning mountain biking ride will take me to Big Rock. Less often I will continue on to Rudy's Flats. The trip to Big Rock will take a reasonably strong rider less than an hour excluding any rest time, while there are those who ride it frequently and can do it in the thirty- to thirty-five-minute range. You should never compare on the trail because there's always a faster and better rider, and just when you think you're pretty hot stuff, someone will come rolling past faster than you can comprehend. My fastest time to Big Rock, of about thirty-one minutes, occurred in the early 2000s when I was riding the trail almost six days a week with my good friend Jeff Zornow. Nowadays on my regular, specialized mountain bike, it takes more like forty-five to fifty minutes. But when I use my more recently acquired assisted-pedal e–mountain bike, it takes twenty-six to twenty-eight minutes.

Much has been discussed in earlier chapters about the ride. Here we will discuss the payoff for any out-and-back rider: the ride down. I love the ride down, especially on a warm day. Sweat from the upward trip cools your body. As rhythm and the trail's undulations pull you along, it's possible to feel that both you and the bike become connected with the track.

Heading down the trail is not all fun and games. It has its own set of requirements necessary to have a positive experience. Since the slope is down most of the time, your posture and center of gravity must be adjusted. This is done by sliding your body back on the seat a few inches while rising slightly so you can take any bumps more smoothly. This is important even with full suspension. Sliding back allows your center of gravity to be slightly farther back over your rear tire, which will help avoid the previously discussed over-the-handlebars flight.

The next set of rules has to do with arms and hands. It's not usually legs or cardio conditioning that requires frequent stops with the less experienced downhill rider; it's the conditioning and strength of the arms, wrists, and hands. The ride down is where this is most evident. A consistently firm grip on the handlebars is critical or else a bump can dislodge the hands, almost always causing an accident.

Carefully focusing ahead on the trail and picking a good line helps, but there are still those moments—a patch of shade hiding a protruding rock or momentum carrying you into a root or loose gravel—that can cause an unexpected problem. Intense hand and forearm isometrics are involved during the seventeen- to twenty-five-minute ride from Big Rock to the parking lot, and longer if you start higher. It's difficult to get that part of your body in shape for this, especially if you're already fatigued after thirty to fifty minutes of uphill riding. It's important to note that the uphill ride can also fatigue your upper body dramatically because of the strength used to pull back on the handlebars as you pump.

Simply gripping the handlebars is not enough; the rider must also constantly be working the brakes. The back brake is the most useful, but careful usage of the front and back brakes in combination is safer and can prevent lockups and skids. Front brake usage must be practiced because improper pressure will lock the front tire and land you on your helmet quicker than anything else. The result is a pair of uninitiated hands that are too fatigued to grip the latch to open the car door when arriving at the bottom of the hill. I remember one particularly difficult ride on Adam's Gulch Loop Trail in Sun Valley, Idaho. Some of the riders had such difficulty with their hands and wrists that it was days before they were able to use them normally again. Wet conditions and damp brakes only make things worse.

Inattentiveness can produce the same results. I was headed down one day and pulled over to the side of the trail to wait for some hikers to pass. I noticed up ahead a young man with headphones on, singing at the top of his lungs and whipping his head around with one hand on the handlebars of his bike while the other held an MP3 player in the air. He was showboating a bit as he rode past some female hikers. I thought of the stretch of roots and rocks that were around the corner about a hundred feet ahead of him. He disappeared around the corner and before I got going again, I heard a loud cry from that direction. Yep, you guessed it—he had hit the rocky area and his showboating antics didn't allow him sufficient grip, so he took a hard spill. By the time I passed him, he was standing again, brushing off the dirt, and talking to himself about where the rocks had come from.

After years of riding, your hands and forearms strengthen and the isometrics are not noticeable, so an experienced guide must carefully watch over his group to make sure they're not having difficulty on the downward trip. There was a time on a family vacation a number of years ago when one of my older teenage nephews and my twenty-something son were having arm wrestling contests. I was in my early fifties at the time and they goaded me into a test. The two were weightlifters, football players, and in top condition. After defeating them three out of four times, both right- and left-handed, one of them asked me the secret of my arm-wrestling prowess. I responded that it was years of gripping the handlebars and brakes while biking. They looked at me with skepticism, and to this day, I think they consider it a fluke. The truth is that it takes tremendous development of hands, wrists, and forearms to comfortably negotiate an uninterrupted trip up and then down a mountain trail.

The Gift of Courtesy

The last area I wish to address here is downhill courtesy. During the euphoria of a downhill run, it's easy to forget you're not on a race course. We can also overlook how hard we worked to get ourselves up the hill.

The International Mountain Biking Association (IMBA) has six well-established rules for mountain riding. Rule number four is "Yield to Others."[34] It briefly references many of the concepts discussed in previous chapters but also includes the counsel that downhill riders should always yield to those going uphill. It further advises that we should strive to make each pass a safe one. On the Mueller Park Trail, this means that the downhill rider needs to communicate ahead and always be able to pull over and step with his bike to the side of the trail so the upward traveler can move past without having to stop or exert additional energy by diverting over rocks, through branches and bushes, or up the side of the trail to get by. Yes, the golden rule is a written part of mountain biking. Those who get lost in their own selfish ride down inconvenience others and, in a worst-case scenario, risk serious accidents and injury.

As we move through life, there are times when we struggle and other times when our passage seems to be surprisingly easy. Of course, we could not appreciate the good times without the periods of adversity. Such conditions are integral to both our individual plan of happiness and our personal salvation. Peter understood the importance of opposition and trial in this life: "That the trial of your faith, being much more precious than of gold that perisheth, though it be tried with fire, might be found unto praise and honour and glory at the appearing of Jesus Christ: Whom having not seen, ye love; in whom, though now ye see him not, yet believing, ye rejoice with joy unspeakable and full of glory: Receiving the end of your faith, even the salvation of your souls" (1 Peter 1:7–9).

The Wise Versus the Foolish

Nephi sheds additional insight and understanding on this:

For it must needs be, that there is an opposition in all things. If not so . . . righteousness could not be brought to pass, neither wickedness, neither holiness nor misery, neither good nor bad. . . .

---

34. "Rules of the Trail," International Mountain Biking Association, accessed Nov. 11, 2024, https://www.imba.com/sites/default/files/Team_IMBA/RulesOfTheTrail.pdf.

CHAPTER 14: THE DOWNHILL RIDE

Wherefore there would have been no purpose in the end of its creation. Wherefore, this thing must needs destroy the wisdom of God and his eternal purposes, and also the power, and the mercy, and the justice of God. . . .

For there could have been no creation of things, neither to act nor to be acted upon; wherefore, all things must have vanished away.

And now, my sons, I speak unto you these things for your profit and learning; for there is a God, and he hath created all things . . . both things to act and things to be acted upon.

And to bring about his eternal purposes in the end of man, after . . . all things which are created, it must needs be that there was an opposition. . . .

Wherefore, the Lord God gave unto man that he should act for himself. Wherefore, man could not act for himself save it should be that he was enticed by the one or the other. (2 Nephi 2:11–16)

As we understand and place in proper perspective both our trials and our blessings, we can more clearly see the necessary eternal balance that alternatively strengthens us and then tests that strength. Making correct, intentional choices moves us forward and upward, ever deepening our roots and enriching our soil as we develop the characteristics of Christ. The result is that we become so much more than we otherwise would have been. This then is the very essence of our journey along the narrow passage of life. We see the culmination of this in the parable of the ten virgins found in the Gospel of Matthew (see Matthew 25:1–13).

In reference to the Second Coming of the Lord (the bridegroom), the parable states that the "kingdom of heaven be likened unto ten virgins, which took their lamps, and went forth to meet the bridegroom. And five of them were wise, and five were foolish" (Matthew 25:1–2). Who are the virgins? They are covenanting believers, or they would not have been invited to meet the bridegroom. Each of them accepted the invitation, yet five, while they clearly believed, were insufficiently prepared, or as John would say, "lukewarm" (Revelation 3:16).

Elder Bruce R. McConkie clarified this when he wrote, "Not good and bad, not righteous and wicked, but wise and foolish. That is, all of them have accepted the invitation to meet the Bridegroom;

all are members of the Church; the contrast is not between the wicked and the worthy. Instead, five are zealous and devoted, while five are inactive and lukewarm; ten have the testimony of Jesus, but only five are valiant therein."[35]

So what was the difference between the wise and foolish virgins in the parable? It was *not* the amount of oil in their lamps, for each virgin had a full lamp of oil at the start. It was the fact that the wise virgins carried with them additional vessels of oil to refill their lamps when they burned low, and the foolish virgins "took no oil with them" (Matthew 25:3). The tragic result for the foolish virgins was that as the evening wore on and the oil in the lamps was consumed, their lamps burned low or went out.

The wise virgins' lamps likewise also burned low, but they re-filled their lamps from the extra vessel they each brought with them. Unfortunately, they did not have enough for the others. The foolish virgins sounded alarmed as they ran to buy additional oil and missed the coming of the bridegroom. The scene at the closed door is heart-breaking as the five believing but foolish virgins returned to find their friends gone and that "the door was shut" (Matthew 25:10). The message is brought home in the bridegroom's answer to the foolish virgin's plea, "saying, Lord, Lord, open to us. But he answered and said, Verily I say unto you, I know you not. Watch therefore, for ye know neither the day nor the hour wherein the Son of man cometh" (Matthew 25:11–13). The Lord further prophesied through Joseph Smith, "And at that day, when I shall come in my glory, shall the parable be ful-filled which I spake concerning the ten virgins. For they that are wise and have received the truth, and have taken the Holy Spirit for their guide, and have not been deceived—verily I say unto you, they shall not be hewn down and cast into the fire, but shall abide the day" (Doctrine and Covenants 45:56–57).

The adversary doesn't need to get us to commit some great sin. He can accomplish his goals by encouraging selfishness, objectification of relationships or loved ones, diversion into paths that go nowhere, and making us vulnerable. He doesn't need to get us to ignore the

---

35. Bruce R. McConkie, *Doctrinal New Testament Commentary* (Deseret Book, 2002), 1:685.

Chapter 14: The Downhill Ride

bridegroom's invitation; rather, simply showing up late or without sufficient oil will do. It seems implicit here that the foolish virgins were not as attuned to the direction of the Holy Ghost as they thought they were.

Satan does not need to destroy us in many cases; we will damn our own progress. Instead of becoming something more, we'll obsessively pursue becoming something less, becoming careless or distracted until we do Satan's work for him in our own lives. Occasionally, we all see those sliding on this misguided path, all the while arguing in their self-focused hubris that they are doing the right thing and growing spiritually closer to God, whose will, counsel, and commandments they have, in fact, chosen to set aside until the door is forever closed.

The Ultimate Phone Call

In 2016 I received a phone call from a woman named Hope, the wife of one of my longtime and dearest friends, Victor Wilcox. They had settled in Austin, Texas, and had married later in life after both having been previously married. Victor and I had become friends in high school while on the same swimming team. We also swam briefly in college together. He was one of the most talented natural swimmers I had ever met, and he continued swimming in the masters competition program into his sixties. He had retired in his late forties after working for years in Switzerland and selling his business. He and Hope traveled actively, climbing, hiking, and generally engaging in challenging outdoor activities. It's safe to say that he had seen most of what this planet had to offer and had been almost everywhere.

Even though he spent a number of years growing up and studying in the Salt Lake City area, he had never seriously investigated the Church. He visited his parents in Utah a couple of times per year and we always got together for lunch, dinner, or a mountain bike ride. About three years before this particular phone call, he and Hope visited and asked if we would take them to Temple Square to show them around. We were happy to do so. We went to dinner at a wonderful local Mexican restaurant, The Blue Iguana, and then did everything we could in the visitor's complex, including the movies, visits to the museums and the family history center, and so on. We were concerned that we might have overdone it a little, but they seemed to thoroughly enjoy the day.

Fast forward to 2016 and the fateful call. Hope explained to me that Vic had developed a brain tumor that had been operated on unsuccessfully and had only weeks to live. I responded by getting a flight to Texas and sitting with him for a couple of days. We watched the Olympic water polo competition and other events during my stay. He couldn't communicate well but we managed. I spent the night in their home, and shortly after Vic had retired to his room, I finally gathered the courage to ask Hope a question that had been burning in my mind since the phone call. I told her I had a request for Vic before he fell asleep that night. She asked me what it was, and I explained that I would like his permission once he passed to do his temple work for him. She asked a few questions about the nature of temple work and what would be done and its purpose. I explained carefully in a way she would understand, I hoped. She agreed to ask him if he would be willing to speak to me about the subject but counseled me to keep the conversation simple and short because he lost focus easily.

She disappeared into Vic's bedroom for a few long minutes, leaving me to my doubts and worry that my last request of Vic would be poorly received. I didn't want our last interaction to be a negative one, so I prayed fervently. Hope returned to the living room and said, "Vic is willing to hear your request." She then showed me to his room. Victor was awake and alert when I entered, and Hope allowed us to have a few private moments. We made some small talk about how nice it was to visit and how deeply grateful he was. Then I asked, "Victor, you know of my deep belief in The Church of Jesus Christ of Latter-day Saints and the work they do in temples for those who have passed on." He nodded his head and slurred the word *yes*. I explained to him that we believe that such covenants made in the temple have an important and powerful impact on us during this life and in the life to come. He nodded again, indicating that Hope had explained some of this to him and that he had picked up over the years some understanding of these matters.

I explained briefly about the ordinances and covenants that we make for ourselves and our kindred dead in the temple and then asked, "Victor, you have been a dear friend most of my life, and I

CHAPTER 14: THE DOWNHILL RIDE

would like to give you the greatest gift I can think of as you prepare for the next life. I ask if you would be willing to allow me personally to do your temple work for you after your passing."

Victor turned his head away from me as he lay on his back in bed. After several long moments that seemed like he was gathering himself for a verbal answer, which was obviously very taxing for him physically, he turned back, looked me in the eyes, and said, "Yes, I would like that very much."

Victor Wilcox passed away just a couple of weeks later, and Hope and I have remained friends. Over the next few months, I went to the Bountiful Temple and acted as proxy for my dear friend as he received his baptism, initiatory, and endowment ordinances. I can tell you that in all my years of serving in the temple, I have never felt the spirit of one for whom I was doing the work so close and present as when I did his work. In my experience, the temple service we do for others is attended personally by those who have chosen to accept the work. They are present and see it happen and know who is doing it for them.

I was fortunate enough to have this experience with my friend and treasure his memory and friendship. I will see him again one day, and we will embrace and celebrate together. This is one way we are asked to serve others that most definitely allows our lamps to be filled with oil. This example of service changed my life and is one of many that each of us has along the way that lead us along the path to becoming.

The oil referred to in the parable is symbolic of something we become—through a life of obedience, service, covenant-making, and the development of a willing mind and heart. It is not just a pathway we fumble along by luck or by random chance. It is our Heavenly Father's strait and narrow path that He will guide us along if we choose to willingly follow. It is a path that, when found, we deliberately and intentionally follow. It cannot be shared; it must grow within you through regular daily and weekly practices and a life of careful spiritual nourishment.

CONCLUDING QUESTIONS TO PONDER

The question is not "What do you have?" Rather, it's "Who have you become?" Put another way, it's not necessarily even who you stand *against* but who you are willing to stand *with*. It's not how you have developed and adorned your outward appearance or position in the community; it is the nature of your heart and the pure love of Christ you have developed.

It is to these the Lord speaks when he says, "Come unto me, all ye that labour and are heavy laden, and I will give you rest. Take my yoke upon you, and learn of me; for I am meek and lowly in heart: and ye shall find rest unto your souls" (Matthew 11:28–29; see also Doctrine and Covenants 54:10). This is the voice I believe my friend, Victor, heard on his last ride down the hill.

15

Why Me?

PLEASE FORGIVE ME AS A WINCE OF PAIN OR SIGH OF FRUSTRATION escapes my lips each time I review this chapter. "Why me?" is a question that is only asked when you find it hard to believe what just happened. Some of the experiences related here and in other places in this book recall feelings that are not pleasant in the moment but are instructive to remember and share. There are two types of experiences on the Mueller Park Trail that evoke such "Why me?" reactions. They fall into the category of accidents and mechanical problems. Both tend to seriously diminish a rider's enjoyment.

Mechanical problems can occur at any time, even if you keep your bike tuned properly. There's a tendency for these problems to occur when you are stressing the bike as well as your body, say up a hill or through a rock field. I remember one morning early in the season. As I stood on my pedals to push up one of the two steep climbs right at the beginning of the ride, my chain snapped. This was not at the expansion link but at the main part of the chain. It was a "turn around and take your bike to the shop" moment.

I have had the expansion link break, which can be managed if you have the right parts, but that's also not fun, and many riders don't carry extra expansion links. On another occasion, my rear brake cable

125

snapped, which didn't end the ride immediately but seriously changed the downhill experience because you can't use the front brake too aggressively without flipping the bike. I also remember my rear shifting cable snapping one morning on the first uphill climb. There are few things as uncomfortable as your gears suddenly shifting to their hardest setting while straining up a steep incline.

There are other mechanical problems that don't end your ride but make things more frustrating, particularly the uphill portion. These tend to be times when the chain has become stretched, or the shifting mechanism is "out of true" and certain gears may pop out or the chain may jump or slip. The "Why me?" occurs because this usually happens when you're pedaling up a slope and really need the extra momentum the most. The slippage can cause such disruption that you can end up off the bike on the ground.

Some of these "Why me?" moments can even be self-inflicted. When riding another's bike on an unfamiliar trail, I reached the top and my thighs were completely worn down to jelly. Upon closer inspection, I discovered that the seat was set one or two inches too low, something I should have noticed earlier but overlooked. With the seat low, it kept me from extending my legs and using the full range of my leg muscles. The effort was therefore limited to my thighs producing poor performance and big-time thigh muscle fatigue. Not fun.

In life, it's easy to identify those who are making their own path gratuitously and unnecessarily more difficult. When you ride with the seat too low, it usually doesn't matter on the flat or downward portions. However, it's significantly more difficult when you hit any uphill climbs. It results in using only your thigh muscles instead of the entire legs, and fatigue sets in much quicker. This is just as true when road biking. I will often come upon a rider who has the seat so low that it looks painful from a couple of hundred yards away. I will sometimes offer a suggestion if they are open to it.

A short seat or a frame that's too small also slows your ride, even if you're not worn out. Those making it harder on themselves rarely recognize the reason for the problem. They simply continue to struggle, thinking that this is how mountain biking is supposed to be. A friendly bit of advice, if they take it, can dramatically change their experience.

CHAPTER 15: WHY ME?

Life is similar. Too many make their lives dramatically more difficult by choosing unwisely. These choices can involve their own selfish pursuits or gratification rather than a well-tested path encouraged by God. They may spend years slogging and struggling while telling themselves this is what life is really supposed to be like. They ignore others passing them by or the joy in others' families or lives, often excusing it or completely ignoring the reasons for it. The decision to "lower your seat" and make it intentionally harder while deceiving yourself accomplishes nothing except wear you out prematurely or force you to miss much of the joy and satisfaction of the journey.

Other problems can be due to a freak circumstance or a combination of unexpected events that produce an accident. Some can be completely unavoidable, while others certainly don't have to happen. One unavoidable situation occurred with me about twenty years ago, and I still watch carefully whenever I pass the spot. Just above the "pipeline," there's a transition from uphill riding to some mostly downhill or level riding. It starts with a steep downhill right curve, and I always call out to make sure other riders are aware around the blind corner. On this day, there were no other riders, so I came around the corner and picked up speed for a brief uphill climb before some nice level rolling. However, I was unaware of a hazard near the ground. There was a thick, leafless branch that was sticking out onto the trail just off the ground, and it became lodged in my front spokes and stopped the rotation of my tire immediately. I was traveling at a good rate, so I did what must have been a beautiful front somersault in near pike position and hit the ground squarely on my head and upper back.

I lay there for a minute or two taking a physical inventory and, yes, wondering "Why me?" I was certainly not the first one on the trail that morning—perhaps a dozen or more riders had passed that spot—but the branch's position was perfect for my tire at that moment. I looked back at my bike and saw that the front rim was bent as well. I took my tire off and pounded it so the wheel would at least turn, but I couldn't get it to the point that it could be ridden. Oh, there's nothing like an extra forty-five-minute walk down the trail to make your day.

Was I blessed in these situations? Yes—because I was not seriously injured. Was the enjoyment of the ride that day ruined or severely diminished? Of course it was. Could similar experiences have ended in serious injury or death? Yes, which has happened to others on the trail before.

As we pass through life, we experience these moments in different ways. There are opportunities along the way to complain, murmur, and even curse God should we choose. They can be particularly difficult if we feel we have been following the Lord's plan and trying to do all we can to obey His will. We may be solidly on the narrow path, firmly grasping the rod of iron, and still experience terrible trials.

Another experience occurred on the Legacy Trail on one of my many twenty-four-mile morning rides. There are some fields with horses and llamas that are fun to ride by, and a couple of small hills arise as you pass the fields. I noted a family walking, except for their very young boy who was riding a small bike. The mother was pushing a stroller, and there were a couple of kids walking and jumping with the dad, generally having a wonderful time together. The boy on the bike was weaving in and out of the broken center line, as many young kids will do, and as I approached, I called out, "Biker coming on your left!" The father and mother heard and pulled their kids toward them for safety, but the boy on the bike didn't respond. I moved over and slowed down, but in his swerving, the boy swerved directly into my front tire. I slammed on my brakes and tried to steer off the trail to avoid him but hit his bike head-on. He was uninjured and his bike was fine; I, however, did another one of those beautiful somersaults over the handlebars, landing on my upper back.

As my vision slowly cleared, I looked up and saw all their faces looking down at me with concern. I was mentally checking my body parts and concluded that scrapes and bruises were the only effects I would be dealing with as a result. As I lay there, the father asked, "Are you all right?" I told him, "I think so." He responded and asked me if I was sure—because he didn't want me suing them later if I decided I was hurt.

I was, in fact, fine and continued my ride a bit wiser. But I wondered in that situation why the father would be mostly worried about whether he would be sued when looking down at me recovering on the ground. In the moment, that's probably all that occurred to him after the shock. No worries—I was fine.

The "Nothing Ever Changes" Trap

We pass through life, sometimes for long periods, without a serious challenge or setback. Our daily routine takes on a "sameness," and we're sometimes lulled into a feeling that every day in the future will repeat the established pattern. This can go on for years. There are the usual bumps in the road, but like mountain biking, they jar us and then pass behind, and then we fall back into our rhythm again and hardly remember. There is little to no indication that a life-changing event is coming just around the corner.

We wake up each day feeling it will be much the same as the day before. Then one day, we awake to the realization that life will never be the same again. The passing of a loved one, serious illness or injury, financial disruption, an earthquake or destructive weather condition, the wandering of a child into strange paths, new or unexpected demands on our time, or a dramatic change in home or family circumstances can all bring this kind of change.

Nephi had one of these days in the wilderness. Lehi and his group were well away from civilization and living off the land. Nephi's hunting prowess was important to their survival. As Nephi "went forth to slay food," he states that he broke his bow, "which was made of fine steel" (1 Nephi 16:18). His brethren were angry and did what they seemed to do best: murmur. It's not hard to imagine the frustration Nephi might have felt. He was responsible, and they were on the Lord's errand following the "directions of the ball" (verse 16). As if the loss of Nephi's bow wasn't enough, his brothers' bows had also become useless, "having lost their springs" (verse 21). Nephi says that it began to be "exceedingly difficult" (verse 21) and that they were not able to obtain any food.

What then did Nephi do? His reaction is not only inspiring but instructive. First, Nephi spoke to his brethren in an effort to address their hard hearts and complaints against God. Then Nephi went about doing what he could to address the problem himself. He made a new bow out of wood and at least one arrow. He also armed himself with a sling and stones and went to his father for guidance.

Here is a man who had received visions and revelations directly from God, but he recognized and respected Lehi's authority and leadership. In addition, this gave Lehi the opportunity to repent, for he had also murmured. Lehi inquired of the Lord, and after he was chastened and humbled, the Lord gave guidance in some writings on the ball. Nephi was directed to "go forth up into the top of the mountain" (1 Nephi 16:30).

Nephi could have reminded the Lord that the children of Israel under Moses had manna every morning outside their tents, and when they tired of manna, they had quail fly right into the camp and fall on the ground (see Exodus 16:13–15). Why couldn't the Lord make a herd of deer or wild boar wander into camp and fall dead at the tent doors? Why did it have to be the top of the mountain? Why not halfway up or in the foothills? These would certainly have been legitimate questions, but this was not Nephi's way, and it's certainly not the Lord's way.

Nephi had set a pattern of seeking to understand the will of the Lord and then doing it. He was told by the Lord, after his father received earlier direction to return for the plates of Laban, that he would "be favored of the Lord, because thou hast not murmured" (1 Nephi 3:6). His philosophy for success was made evident in his response to Lehi, saying, "I will go and do the things which the Lord hath commanded, for I know that the Lord giveth no commandments unto the children of men, save he shall prepare a way for them that they may accomplish [them]" (1 Nephi 3:7). The result of Nephi's obedience and faith was a successful hunt and rejoicing by the entire family.

The book of Ruth tells us of a woman named Naomi who traveled with her husband and two sons to the land of Moab. This displacement occurred because of a famine in their homeland of Judah. While in this strange land, Naomi's husband died. This was, of course, an unspeakably difficult time; however, she still had her two sons who took wives of the women of Moab and together cared for their mother. Unfortunately, after some time, both of Naomi's sons died, leaving the three women alone. Naomi, a kind and loving mother-in-law, released her daughters-in-law from any obligation and determined to return to her people in Judah.

One daughter-in-law, Ruth, chose to stay with Naomi. Naomi attempted to talk Ruth out of it by explaining her poor prospect of finding a husband in a strange land with no kinfolk and different beliefs.

However, Ruth would not hear of it. Her response contains no "Why me?" voice at all: "And Ruth said, Entreat me not to leave thee, or to return from following after thee: for whither thou goest, I will go; and where thou lodgest, I will lodge: thy people shall be my people, and thy God my God: Where thou diest, will I die, and there will I be buried: the Lord do so to me, and more also, if ought but death part thee and me" (Ruth 1:16–17). When Naomi saw that Ruth was "steadfastly minded to go with her, then she left speaking unto her" (Ruth 1:18). Of course, the rest of the story is that Ruth was blessed for her faithfulness, she eventually married into the line of Judah, and through her direct lineage was born King David (see Ruth 4:17).

What did Ruth do? Her reaction, like Nephi's, is inspiring. First, there's no indication that she was consumed with self-victimization upon the loss of her husband. Then Ruth demonstrated her willingness to be selfless by putting Naomi's well-being first. She followed faithfully without murmur or complaint. Here is a woman who was by all outward appearances ordinary. She had different beliefs and was going to a strange land in a situation where, by tradition, her prospects for a better life as a widow were bleak. Yet she went without question or hesitation and in spite of resistance from Naomi.

Would it have been understandable if Ruth had cursed her situation, complained to God, or returned to the safety of life with her kinsmen? Of course. But she demonstrated that rare and wonderful quality found in all the great and faithful leaders of scripture. She had faith in God and an unflinching willingness to follow His will, even if expressed indirectly through others. When presenting herself before Boaz, she was told by Naomi to follow some specific instructions, and what was her answer? "All that thou sayest unto me I will do" (Ruth 3:5).

Herein we find plain and simple examples of how to deal with life's great trials. In contrast, Laman and Lemuel's murmuring behavior and the children of Israel's constant complaints to Moses make plain to us what *not* to do. Faithful disciples pray for protection, guidance, inspiration, and to prosper in the land, and certainly many would be justified in receiving such. That doesn't mean we can't inquire of the Lord or ask questions. In fact, we are encouraged to do so. But *which* questions we ask makes a difference.

Life doesn't always go smoothly. Our ability to provide for our families is sometimes interrupted. Famine or economic upheavals can strike unexpectedly. We may be commanded to do things that are difficult or seem impossible, and sometimes we find ourselves in situations where we can't figure out how to begin.

Imagine Moses when he was first commanded to lead his people out of bondage. He had already been exiled from Egypt and was essentially a nomad in the wilderness. He was slow of speech and believed himself to be a "nobody" (see Exodus 3:11, 13; 4:1, 10). Or perhaps we can imagine ourselves in the position of Nephi when he was commanded to build a ship to carry his growing family group across the great oceans. He was a city boy, not a seafarer. He was commanded to go up into a mountain and was given the task of building a ship. He made one request, which seemed legitimate since he was in an unfamiliar land—he asked to know where he might find ore that he might make tools (see 1 Nephi 17:7–9). Yet in both cases—Moses's and Nephi's—they obeyed, trusted in the Lord, and went about their duties without complaint.

In these cases, there was earthly deliverance, but that's not always so. Stephen was not delivered from those who wished to stone him (see Acts 7:54–60). Abinadi was burned before King Noah (see Mosiah 17:20). Abel was not delivered from Cain (see Genesis 4:8). Jonathan was not delivered from death on Mount Gilboa (see 2 Samuel 1:21–23). John the Baptist was not delivered from Herod (see Mark 6:27). The mob at Carthage was not prevented from martyring Joseph and Hyrum (see Doctrine and Covenants 135:1). Neither were many of the early Apostles, including Paul, James, and Peter delivered from their fates. Brigham Young was not given a completed railroad to Utah upon which the Saints could travel.

What then can we learn from these apparent contradictions?

"But If Not"

Elder Dennis E. Simmons gave us wise counsel in dealing with such situations:

> The Lord has given us agency, the right and the responsibility to decide. He tests us by allowing us to be challenged. . . . But we

CHAPTER 15: WHY ME?

must understand that great challenges make great men. We don't seek tribulation, but if we respond in faith, the Lord strengthens us. The *but if nots* can become remarkable blessings. . . .

Our God will deliver us from ridicule and persecution, *but if not*. . . . Our God will deliver us from sickness and disease, *but if not* . . . He will deliver us from loneliness, depression, or fear, *but if not*. . . . Our God will deliver us from threats, accusations, and insecurity, *but if not*. . . . He will deliver us from death or impairment of loved ones, *but if not, . . . we will trust in the Lord.*[36]

He continues, "Our God will see that we receive justice and fairness, *but if not*. . . . He will make sure that we are loved and recognized, *but if not*. . . . We will receive a perfect companion and righteous and obedient children, *but if not . . . we will have faith in the Lord Jesus Christ, knowing that if we do all we can do, we will, in His time and in His way, be delivered and receive all that He has.*"[37]

Trials that seem contrary to our righteous prayers and efforts do not necessarily mean we're doing something wrong. We're here on this earth to have a collection of growth experiences—to face opposition and temptation and through those things develop and exercise faith and make correct choices that move us closer to God. This can't happen if our life is completely devoid of any challenge or trial. It's the very nature of this earth life that allows us to have those days that we wonder "Why me?" or "Why now, just when things were going so well?" or "Why now, when things are already so difficult?"

The answer is that God has a plan designed to refine and develop us spiritually into persons who will be worthy and willing to dwell with Him and our Savior and do the eternal work they have prepared for the faithful. Refinement is uncomfortable. Preparation takes action and time. But the path is clear. Jacob counsels us to "come unto the Lord, the Holy One. . . . Behold, the way for man is narrow, but it lieth in a straight course before him, and the keeper of the gate is the Holy One of Israel; and he employeth no servant there; and there is none other way save it be by the gate; for he cannot be deceived, for the Lord God is his name" (2 Nephi 9:41). The Savior Himself

---

36. Dennis E. Simmons, "But if Not . . .," *Ensign* or *Liahona*, May 2004, 73–75.

37. Dennis E. Simmons, "But if Not . . .," 75.

commanded us to "enter ye in at the strait gate: for wide is the gate, and broad is the way, that leadeth to destruction, and many there be which go in thereat: Because strait is the gate, and narrow is the way, which leadeth unto life, and few there be that find it" (Matthew 7:13–14).

There are times in each of our lives when we are driven to our knees with seemingly overwhelming burdens or with sorrow that comes from a deep place in our heart and bursts out in a wail of agony. These days can bring us to the edge of a deep abyss where we cry out for help and feel we cannot take another step and would that we could let this cup pass from our lips. These are times when we speak in the midst of unbearable sorrow and our Father knows that we would consent to being taken if it were His will.

Moses had one of these days when the children of Israel tormented him because they were tired of manna and demanded meat. He cried to the Lord, "I am not able to bear all this people alone, because it is too heavy for me. And if thou deal thus with me, kill me, I pray thee, out of hand, if I have found favour in thy sight; and let me not see my wretchedness" (Numbers 11:14–15). Our spirits may be racked with responsibilities we feel we cannot bear, with torment, with sorrow, with physical or spiritual pain, or with fear as we question if there's any hope at all. There are days when we cannot in the morning see how we will survive to the evening. A loving Heavenly Father has not left us alone, for He promises to give "power to the faint; and to them that have no might He increaseth strength" (Isaiah 40:29).

The cause of the moment when our spirit reaches a tipping point isn't as important as what we do with it. For it is in those moments that we can also feel the Spirit of the Lord's love wash over us like cool water on a hot day. The calming comes, the trembling stops, and then we hear the words of our Savior and Friend, "Love one another, as I have loved you. Greater love hath no man than this, that a man lay down his life for his friends. Ye are my friends" (John 15:12–14).

We are comforted as Joseph Smith was when in one of his darkest hours, the Lord spoke to him, saying, "Know thou, my son, that all these things shall give thee experience, and shall be for thy good. . . . Therefore, hold on thy way, and the priesthood shall remain with thee" (Doctrine and Covenants 122:7–9).

The Doctrine of Nevertheless

Our minds may well be called to remember the Savior's example in the garden when He prayed with exceeding sorrow, even unto, death to let this cup pass from Him but concluded with the powerful resolution of faith in his Father's plan, "Nevertheless not as I will, but as thou wilt" (Matthew 26:39). Thus is revealed the great doctrine of "nevertheless" known to the faithful throughout history. We may face darkness, fear, anxiety, shame, threat, a looming need for repentance, or the evil intentions of those who would take from us everything of worth. *Nevertheless*, we do all we can to persevere, stand fast, and take another step forward. The peace and calm are waiting to wash over us. Ralph Waldo Emerson knew this great promise when he said, "A hero is no braver than an ordinary man, but he is brave five minutes longer."[38]

Can we give our loving Father and His Son Jesus five more minutes? We can try. We may feel to exclaim with Alma, "Behold, when I thought this, I could remember my pains no more; yea, I was harrowed up by the memory of my sins no more. And oh, what joy, and what marvelous light I did behold; yea, my soul was filled with joy as exceeding as was my pain! Yea, I say unto you . . . that there could be nothing so exquisite and so bitter as were my pains. Yea . . . on the other hand, there can be nothing so exquisite and sweet as was my joy" (Alma 36:19–21). In these quiet moments, we may understand some small part that our Savior felt when He prayed that the cup could pass from His lips but then, in the crowning submission of all history, said, "Nevertheless not as I will, but as thou wilt" (Matthew 26:39).

He is our Friend, we are loved, and He laid down his life for us for a purpose. That purpose is that we might overcome and return to God and be with Him again. These are times when we come to know God and feel Christ's unconditional love for us. As we are encircled by the Spirit, we understand that we're not forgotten, we have a reason for being, we have value beyond measure, and we have never been alone.

---

38. Ralph Waldo Emerson, "A Hero Is No Braver," BrainyQuote, accessed Nov. 11, 2024, https://www.brainyquote.com/quotes/ralph_waldo_emerson_104751.

16

It's a Beautiful Day for a Ride

IT'S 6:30 AM ON A SATURDAY MORNING IN JULY, AND ALL IS QUIET AS I roll out of bed. I step out the front door to get a sense of the temperature and weather. Quietly I put on my riding shorts, a T-shirt, and my riding jersey, grab my helmet and sunglasses, and give my sweetheart a kiss on the cheek. She knows I will be back by about 8:15 a.m., ready to get going with the regular responsibilities we have planned for the day.

After checking air pressure, hydrating, and filling my water bottle with ice and water, I'm on my way up to the trailhead. The morning is still cool, but I know it will become much warmer as the sun rises. I do one more check of my brakes, lock my rear shock, stretch a bit, and ride the short distance to the trailhead from my parking spot to help loosen up. Stopping at the trailhead, there are, as usual, about a dozen cars already having expelled their occupants. The cars sit patiently awaiting the return of their masters.

It's clear that some bikers and walkers are already on the hill, so I take a mental note to make sure I call out my approach on the blind corners. After a few more moments of stretching (I find I need that more with age) and setting my bike meter and timer, off I go. I cross the bridge and gather momentum for the first two climbs, standing up as I approach them. It goes smoothly, and I stay in the gears I had planned. The ride continues to rise through the first two sharp switchbacks and then around what I call "big bend," which is another stand-up pedal stretch. A few minutes later, I approach the first outlook. It's a gorgeous, clear day and I'm about a third of the way to Big Rock.

I've passed a couple of walkers on their way up, and an early-bird biker or two have come by on their way down. The downhill bikers don't call out, but luckily, I come upon them on one of the straight stretches so there are no problems. I notice fresh, slightly deeper, tire tracks in the dust, which indicates that bikers are not too far ahead of me going up. The deeper tracks are always from riders pumping hard as they ascend the hill. I use it for motivation to keep up my pace and try to catch them.

I approach the first inside curve and gain a little bit of downhill momentum for the first time in the ride, then there's another long outside climb to a series of four small rises that I call the roller coaster coming down. Visibility is good from here to the second inside turn and the halfway mark (in time) of the ride. I'm at about eighteen to twenty-two minutes, which is pretty good for me nowadays (although I recall that when I rode the trail more often twenty-four years ago, I would reach this point two to three minutes earlier). Another outside uphill climb and two more beautiful scenic view spots before I head for the last inside turn before the "pipeline."

There are two pipelines nowadays, and you cross the clear-cut for the newer one first. But when I refer to the "pipeline," it's always the older and first pipeline farther up the hill. The climb from the third inside turn to the pipeline is one of the most technical parts of the trail and includes split levels, some more steep stretches, and a final uphill stretch through a rock field that requires momentum and a proper line to negotiate without touching. I don't like to touch down—it means momentum is gone, and plus, with some of my riding buddies, a foot touch means you lose credibility points.

I make it around the outside curve to the pipeline and find a group of bikers resting and enjoying the view. (This is a place where the underground Kern River Pipeline crosses the trail, and you can clearly see where the foliage was cut away over thirty-five years ago to bury the pipe.) Many stop here to catch their breath after the tough

CHAPTER 16: IT'S A BEAUTIFUL DAY FOR A RIDE

stretch. But I continue on, knowing that after one more brief uphill push, there's a nice portion of flat to downward rolling.

The first downward roll is around a sharp blind corner. Every year, riders approach this too quickly or without calling out, and there are accidents or places where they skid off the trail, eating away at the trail width right at the critical corner stretch. It's about a foot wide here now because there are already spots where bikers have torn away parts of the trail by skidding out of control. I call out and gain momentum for a good uphill stretch to the next inside turn. It was at this point twenty years ago that I surprised a juvenile moose in the spring. It was as large as a horse and trotted ahead of me on the trail until the next inside turn, then lumbered up into the trees without looking back.

The trail is now faster, rolling, and relatively level except for one little uphill that can have the consistency of gluey mud if there has been rain lately. The key to this thirty-foot muddy stretch is to keep your momentum and not have to pedal so hard that you spin your tires. This avoids a very messy dismount and a walk to a dry spot. It's dry today, so I stand and pedal up through the trees, calling out again for the next turn. The outside turn here is heavy with foliage on both sides, which masks the steep drop-offs to the left and requires calling out frequently due to restricted sight.

I cross a very short bridge, which is also on a blind corner, and approach the first long, wide bridge on the trail. It's a beautiful spot where walkers with dogs often stop so their dogs can be refreshed. It's the first water since the trailhead, about thirty minutes into the ride. The approaches to both ends of the bridge were rebuilt by my son Travis and his friend Reggie about twenty-six years ago for his friend's Eagle project. It remained in pretty good condition for years but has recently been upgraded. It took them many hours to haul the railroad ties to this location for the work to repair the approaches. I think about it every time I cross this bridge.

After crossing the bridge, there's a steep and always wet uphill push, then another narrower bridge that requires a six- to eight-inch hop to get onto. The bridge is so narrow that if you lose your balance, it's likely you'll end up lying sideways in a marshy, spring-fed creek that runs under the bridge. I build momentum and stand up for the hop with no problem. (There's a rock just before the bridge that helps you ramp up right onto the higher level if you hit it just right.)

The trail then winds to another outside turn and more relatively level riding. I pass the flat-sided rock (that catapulted me off the trail some years ago and down a hundred-foot rockslide) and notice it's still there, reminding me that I should remain aware and focused now that I'm approaching the end of the uphill ride to Big Rock and am feeling fatigued.

There are very steep, long drop-offs to the left all along the trail here and some slick, flat-angled rocks to cross. Keeping balance and focusing ahead is important in this stretch. There's a slight uphill part, a blind right turn, and a fifty- to sixty-foot narrow bridge that can't accommodate passing. A huge porcupine that lives under or near this bridge is occasionally observed on the trail in this area. I approach and cross the last inside turn, which also has a bridge crossing a small stream. The trail then climbs again to a steep outside turn that has another rock field. I pick my usual outside line, stand up, and pump to get around the rocky bend ahead and prepare for a difficult hop over a large tree root across the trail, complicated by a rock on the right side. This spot is only about four inches wide and allows no margin for error, and the hop must be just right or you get another dismount and little walk. After surmounting the last material obstacle, it's a gradual uphill climb for another two hundred feet to Big Rock and I'm done. I coast my bike around the corner and lay it down near the bench where several travelers already sit.

I have a curved root to the side that I love to sit down on, and I do so after stretching my hamstrings and calves. I will usually call my wife, if it's not too early, and tell her I made it safely to the rock one more time and when to expect me home. A few mornings, I'll call to harass one of my riding buddies, usually a son, about sleeping in instead of coming up the hill. Some pleasant conversation with other morning travelers and a beautiful view make the morning fantastic, and it's not even 7:30 a.m. yet.

I mount my bike, unlock the rear shock (I prefer to hard-tail it up the hill) and head down, keeping a reasonable speed so as to avoid inconveniencing those coming up. A few walkers and a rider have unleashed dogs, which cause some problems for other trail users, but

Chapter 16: It's a Beautiful Day for a Ride

I dismount and allow them to pass. There are also an increasing number of people with earbuds in, and I'm always glad I learned to whistle loudly without using my fingers when I was a young boy. I need that whistle every single day on both the mountain and the road trails.

There are many more on the trail on the lower stretches, and by the time I get to the trailhead, there are even more getting started. (Many who use the trail seem to arrive between 8:00 and 8:30 a.m. on these days.)

My ride completed, I load the bike on the back of my truck, check for any new scrapes or damage (I notice a new cut on my shin from a branch on the way down), and drive home. Another beautiful day has started with a great experience. I overlook the strain and challenge of the ride and focus on the feeling of accomplishment, the exercise, and the enjoyment.

Mixed-Bag Journeys

Our daily experience away from the mountain can be the same. Each day is a mixed bag of challenges, tasks, disappointments, and accomplishments. Life doesn't seem to neatly organize such experiences. They come mixed up and often piled upon each other. My mission president once told me that his days were almost always like that. He would go from an uplifting interview with a bright-eyed new convert preparing for baptism, immediately to the next interview, perhaps with a missionary having serious problems, anxiety, or homesickness who simply wants to quit and go home. Our spiritual development along the way prepares us for these dramatic highs and lows that often come in rapid succession.

By focusing on our overall progress, staying close to our spiritual guides, and engaging in daily nourishment, we learn to love those with whom we are traveling on this exceptional adventure. We can find inner strength, rest, peace, and joy no matter what each day brings. Perhaps even more importantly, we are able to have this spiritual strength abundantly enough that we can impart it to others with whom we counsel.

My rides up the mountain remind me of this and how blessed I am—not just to be able to sit on the bench at Big Rock one more time but also to share the accomplishments of each day with a loving Father in Heaven, a wonderful companion, and family, which make every step along the way worthwhile.

Epilogue: How to Identify a Mountain Biker

WHEN PLANNING A RIDE ALONG EITHER THE NARROW PATH OR A mountain single track, it's important to have an experienced guide, as was discussed in some detail in chapter 4. It's both short-sighted and potentially dangerous to go alone, especially if you're unfamiliar with the track. Choosing proper earthly trail guides is important. How do we identify them? Some assistance can again be provided by our comparison to mountain biking. It's difficult to identify a quality guide if all you plan to do is stand in the middle of a busy sidewalk and watch people passing by. You can get some indication from their outward appearance, of course, but less obvious indications tell the real story.

One sure way to tell an experienced mountain biker is to look at his shins and the back and sides of his calves. Why? As you can tell from many of the experiences included in this book, there are times during almost every ride when you need to dismount quickly. With any quick mount or dismount, there's a likelihood that the pedals or sprocket will catch the front or back of your legs. This usually leaves sprocket-shaped grease marks, scrapes or scratches, some cuts, and by the end of the season, telltale scars. I say this a bit tongue-in-cheek, but any experienced rider can relate. This also leads us to

143

The Battle for Souls Continues

There is no question that this earth is a battleground. There has been a war waged for the souls of men since the dim reaches of our existence prior to this life. Satan is the leader of the opposition. He is just as real as God. His forces are organized, relentless, and always awake and working. We overcame the premortal rebellion of Satan and kept the first estate spoken of by Jude and Abraham (see Jude 1:6; Abraham 3:26, 28), and we earned the right to come to this earth to gain bodily temples and develop faith. Because of this, we are Satan's targets.

There are forces for righteousness arrayed on our side. Those forces include our Heavenly Father, Jesus Christ, the Holy Ghost, angelic hosts commissioned to minister and protect mankind, the writings of prophets and inspired individuals long passed on, individuals among us who are called to specific prophetic assignments today, and others who are called by the Spirit into our path. God works His marvelous work and wonder through all these resources and more (see Isaiah 29:14). Righteous forces will ultimately triumph, but at what cost in human souls, pain, suffering, and personal loss we cannot begin to imagine.

One thing that can be said with certainty is that none of us will pass this way unscathed. Many of the prophets have suffered mightily in the wilderness or during trials. Joseph of Egypt suffered at the hands of his brothers (see Genesis 37:28) and at the hand of Potiphar unjustly (Genesis 39:20). Even though the end of Joseph's story was a happy one, and clearly the process and result were part of God's plan to preserve the family of Jacob for great things, Joseph surely suffered mightily along the way.

Even the "sons of Helaman" were not immune to the effects of this great eternal battle when they faced their trials. Helaman tells us that after one of the most fearsome battles, "after the Lamanites had fled, I immediately gave orders that my men who had been wounded should be taken from among the dead, and caused that their wounds should be dressed. And . . . there were two hundred, out of my two thousand and sixty, who had fainted because of the loss of blood; nevertheless, according to the goodness of God . . . there was not one soul of them who did perish; yea, and neither was there one soul among them who had not received many wounds" (Alma 57:24–25).

The young Ammonites had faithful mothers and fathers who had cultivated their deep roots, and they had a loving leader in Helaman who they referred to as a father. They had the faith that comes from growing up in righteous homes, and Helaman records that even though they had never before fought, not a single one of them died in the battle even while thousands around them were slain (see Alma 57:26). That, however, does not mean they didn't suffer severely from the fight. As mentioned, each one had suffered wounds.

We too can become injured and faint from the battles we are called to fight. But we have been given the armor of God to protect us if we choose to strap it on and keep it clean and pure (see Ephesians 6:10–18; Doctrine and Covenants 27:15–18). Properly chosen guides can help us keep our armor in pristine condition and teach us how to use it wisely. The young Ammonites learned to obey their mothers and trusted in them such that they followed the Lord's direction with unquestioning faith and exactness (see Alma 57:21).

Joseph clearly was taught obedience, hard work, and trust by his parents and God. These qualities were refined by the fires of great trial. Such qualities are found in not only the great scriptural leaders and prophets but in all those who serve as God commanded Solomon: "And thou, Solomon my son, know thou the God of thy father, and serve him with a perfect heart and with a willing mind: for the Lord searcheth all hearts, and understandeth all the imaginations of the thoughts: if thou seek him, he will be found of thee; but if thou forsake him, he will cast thee off for ever" (1 Chronicles 28:9). These are the ones to whom the Lord has said, "Ask, and it shall be given you; seek, and ye shall find; knock, and it shall be opened unto you: For every one that asketh receiveth; and he that seeketh findeth; and to him that knocketh it shall be opened" (Matthew 7:7–8; see also Doctrine and Covenants 4:7). But they did not stand alone. Each one of us has been given that same promise by the Savior Himself.

Seek Knowledge from Sources Who Know

You may have noted frequent references to the scriptures. One way to maintain your momentum and preparation for any path is to seek knowledge from inspired guides who know the path. One of the great failings in modern society is that too many look everywhere except the best sources. It makes no sense to spend your time studying a book by someone who hates mountain biking to find out about the subject. We all too often find those who are wandering on strange paths who only look to those who disdain religion or a particular book of scripture or belief. Hate and contention toward any subject prevent learning and teaching. It's far better to work with a guide who knows and loves the sport and path because they have tried it for themself and can speak authoritatively rather than spout hearsay and talking points or repeat titillating rumors.

The Man in the Arena

There's one other quality that Ruth and the young Ammonites shared with great men like Abraham, Moses, Joseph, Nephi, Ammon, Mormon, Moroni, Peter, Paul, Joseph Smith, Brigham Young, and others. It's developed in not only the great scriptural writers and prophets but in all those who serve with all their "heart, might, mind and strength" (Doctrine and Covenants 4:2). These individuals recognized the same principle taught by Teddy Roosevelt at the Paris Sorbonne University over a hundred years ago. One brief portion of his address makes the point precisely.

> It is not the critic who counts: not the man who points out how the strong man stumbles or where the doer of deeds could have done better. The credit belongs to the man who is actually in the arena, whose face is marred by dust and sweat and blood, who strives valiantly, who errs and comes up short again and again, because there is no effort without error or shortcoming, but who knows the great enthusiasms, the great devotions, who spends himself in a worthy cause; who, at the best, knows, in the end, the triumph of high achievement, and who, at the worst, if he fails, at least he fails while

Epilogue: How to Identify a Mountain Biker

daring greatly, so that his place shall never be with those cold and timid souls who knew neither victory nor defeat.[39]

Contemplating this statement provides thoughtful insight into who we really are and where we need to stand. It reinforces that there are three kinds of people in the world today. The first two types we find on the arena floor, some motivated by righteous goals and others striving for selfish, hateful, wicked, and evil results. These two groups are engaging in a fight that will change the future for others in the world. They are doing all they can to bring about change for either good or evil. They know where they are and are taking action.

The third group includes those sitting in the bleachers. They cheer, critique, observe, and occasionally move about to get a better seat closer to the action or move farther away. These are the critics—they may know all the key statistics of those in the arena, but they do not make a difference. They do not act; rather, their eternal situation is determined by their own inaction and by the actions of others on the floor of the arena. The Lord refers to these as being "acted upon" (2 Nephi 2:14, 26).

Yet many in this third group sincerely believe that by observing, they are accomplishing something when they are not. Some even campaign in their own self-important belief that others should follow them to their special seating area in the stands. It's an effective tool of the adversary to convince them that they're doing something when they are not, that they have enough oil when they do not, or that they are sufficiently prepared when there is still much to do.

He tells them that a little distraction doesn't hurt, a little lie or taking advantage of others can be justified, and in the end, everything will be okay because they didn't really do anything seriously wrong (see 2 Nephi 28:7–9). Yet those who spend their lives in selfish self-entertainment and distraction never become what they could be and in eternity will find themselves falling far short: "I know thy works, that thou art neither cold nor hot: I would thou wert cold or hot. So then because thou art lukewarm, and neither cold nor hot, I will spue

---

39. Theodore Roosevelt, "It Is Not the Critic Who Counts [Speech at the Sorbonne, Paris, April 23, 1910]," Theodore Roosevelt Conservation Partnership, Jan. 18, 2011, https://www.trcp.org/2011/01/18/it-is-not-the-critic-who-counts/.

thee out of my mouth" (Revelation 3:15–16). They find themselves returning "again to their own place, to enjoy that which they are willing to receive, because they were not willing to enjoy that which they might have received. For what doth it profit a man if a gift is bestowed upon him, and he receive not the gift?" (Doctrine and Covenants 88:32–33).

Do Something Worth Doing

We are not only commanded to "obey" and "refrain from"; more importantly, we're commanded to "do" (James 1:22) many good and worthwhile things to help bring to pass God's work and our own becoming. And what is God's great love and work? "For God so loved the world, that he gave his only begotten Son, that whosoever believeth in him should not perish, but have everlasting life. For God sent not his Son into the world to condemn the world; but that the world through him might be saved" (John 3:16–17). In these verses, Jesus tells us of the great work that is His and Heavenly Father's that we might "have everlasting life." Our Heavenly Father loved each of us so much that He created a plan that would allow us to come to earth, grow, make choices, repent, overcome our mistakes, and return to Him. This plan required His Son, even our Savior, Jesus Christ, as a sacrifice to pay the price for our mistakes, transgressions, and sins. This is the greatest demonstration of that godly love. It witnesses beyond question the importance of such work for each of us. We are His work! (See Moses 1:39.)

This requires those who count themselves as sincere believers to be in the arena fighting the good fight. It's imperative that each person be absolutely positive that they are fighting on God's side because Satan is a master at deception and counterfeit and is able to mislead even those who see themselves as devout (see Matthew 24:24). It's not necessary for us to be the greatest warriors in the fight, but it is necessary that we give all we have and do all we can.

Yes, those of us on the arena floor will stumble; we will be wounded time and again, experience a loss of blood, and even be dislocated from our planned line of travel once in a while. But we will be fighting valiantly, and we will not be alone. That is what's meant when

Epilogue: How to Identify a Mountain Biker

the psalmist tells us, "Yea, though I walk through the valley of the shadow of death, I will fear no evil: for thou art with me; thy rod and thy staff they comfort me" (Psalm 23:4). Nephi tells us, "I was led by the Spirit, not knowing beforehand the things which I should do. Nevertheless I went forth" (1 Nephi 4:6–7), and "We labor diligently to write, to persuade our children, and also our brethren, to believe in Christ, and to be reconciled to God; for we know that it is by grace that we are saved, after all we can do" (2 Nephi 25:23).

It is this effort to diligently understand the Lord's will and then do it, even though we may fear and tremble at times, that helps us become the kind of person who will want to come unto Him. As a good mountain biker is able to achieve the desired results by following basic principles, so also can we achieve desirable results along life's narrow path. The result is worth it, as promised in the scriptures: "The Lord is my shepherd, I shall not want. He maketh me to lie down in green pastures: he leadeth me beside the still waters. He restoreth my soul: he leadeth me in the paths of righteousness. . . . Thou anointest my head with oil; my cup runneth over. . . . Surely goodness and mercy shall follow me all the days of my life: and I will dwell in the house of the Lord forever" (Psalm 23:1–6). As Alma promised, "Ye shall reap the rewards of your faith, and your diligence, and patience, and long-suffering, waiting for the tree to bring forth fruit unto you" (Alma 32:43).

This, my friends, is worth the fight. It doesn't matter where you start from or how mistake-filled or rebellious your life has been up to now. God and His servants will come to you where you are and walk with you from there. He will start with you from where you are—not from where you're supposed to be or from where others think you should be, but from where you really are. He knows and is unafraid, and we should be unafraid as well.

Come and let us make these principles a part of our souls and ride together with a worthy guide. I will ever be there standing at the trailhead beckoning you to follow. Our Lord and Savior, Jesus Christ, will walk with you on your journey. He will also be there at the end of the trail, arms outstretched, ready to embrace you and say as He did to those who multiplied their talents regardless of how many talents resulted, "Well done, thou good and faithful servant: thou hast been faithful over a few things, I will make thee ruler over many things: enter thou into the joy of thy lord" (Matthew 25:21).

Acknowledgments

MY ORIGINAL WORK TITLED *LIFE ON THE NARROW PATH* WAS PUBLISHED well over a decade ago. It was directed toward the general Christian audience based on the broader market potential and advice from my publisher. Since then, so much has changed in the world. Attacks on the younger generation have never been so openly and brazenly promoted. It is well past time for some significant editing to the original book with extensive new material added specifically designed for those who have or are struggling with their faith and wondering how their membership in The Church of Jesus Christ of Latter-day Saints fits in today's world.

How do I begin to share my gratitude for the marathon that occurs between the first glimmer of thought to the finished and published work? While it's an impossible task to adequately address, I wish to recognize a few who have made a difference in this process. I must first thank my riding buddies over the years: Jeff Zornow; Dan Sellers; Jonathan Butler; sons Travis, Howie, and Neil; a daughter, Maren; daughters-in-law Ellie and Shaunna; various friends John Peterson, Keith West, Paul Haliday, Victor Wilcox, Lisa and Creighton Rider, and Todd and Karin Cook; and my sweetheart, Leah, as well as numerous others, including an entire new generation of awesome grandchildren—Christopher, Courtney, Carson, Callie, Jack, Noah, and more to come—for inspiration, conversation, friendship, and occasional first aid along the countless single-track and road rides taken together. I should also give a shout-out to all my friends who are part of Creighton's Riders.

Riding is first and foremost a social experience for me as well as a way to stay fit and alive so that I can continue my ministry here on this earth. On the trail, most people are courteous, quick to stop to render assistance, and friendly.

In updating and revising *A Saint's Journey on the Narrow Path*, I have drawn from my own journals and experiences as well as a volume of other annotated sources. I especially appreciate Emily Clark of Cedar Fort Publishing & Media for encouraging me to take the steps to prepare this book for publication and for her support and ideas in getting things kicked off. I have long thought it necessary and important to prepare this more focused version of my advice and insights for spiritual growth during these troubled times we currently live in. I'm especially grateful to Bryce Mortimer, CEO of Cedar Fort, for believing in this material and how it can be used to inspire souls in that critical age group of teens through thirty-somethings. Thanks also to the entire staff at Cedar Fort whose tireless work has brought into reality this exciting new resource to reach and gather souls to Christ.

I cannot adequately express my thanks and love for each one of my children, who have brought such joy to my life. Whether or not we are in regular contact, they need to know that my love and gratitude for them has never diminished. To my parents, now passed on, who set me on the path and encouraged my progress even if they were unable to follow until later in life, I say thank you for teaching me to never give up on my dreams. And to my sweetheart, Leah, who loves without condition, gives without expectation of return, prays without ceasing, and provided tipping-point encouragement with this new edition of Mountain Biker Parables—there certainly would be no book and likely no mountain biker to write it without you. Your smile and encouragement launched this effort and have kept it on track when hope seemed unreachable. You exemplify all the best traits of a "good guide."

ACKNOWLEDGMENTS

Finally, I cannot move on without expressing heartfelt appreciation to my Heavenly Father and my Savior, Jesus Christ, who, through the influence and ministration of the Spirit, have been there during my darkest days to let me know I was never alone and that there were blessings in store beyond my wildest dreams. They have guided my hand and research in producing this work, and it is to Them that I owe all that I have and all that I am. Thank you.

About the Author

CLARK RICH BURBIDGE GREW UP IN THE HIGH MOUNTAIN VALLEYS of the Rockies. His high school experience included instrumental and vocal music as well as varsity participation in football and swimming. He attended college at the University of Utah where he competed in two varsity sports with letters in swimming and water polo. Clark grew up in a loving family, and even though they didn't actively participate in the Church until much later in his life, he was mentored by many along the way and found his own conversion at age 19. He served in the Massachusetts Boston Mission under Allen C. and Dawna Rozsa, who he had the opportunity to work closely with and who became a guiding light for him as he learned and grew.

He has since served in a vast number of responsibilities in the Church for over fifty years. His service has usually found him working extensively with youth and young adults. He and his sweetheart are currently on assignment at the Utah State Correctional Facility where they have served for nearly three years. They help staff one of the Church's organized branches at the prison and are also called as service missionaries with special emphasis on leading addiction recovery and self-reliance classes for male and female inmates, including those with mental health conditions.

Clark's career spanned over thirty-five years in finance as a corporate and investment banker and more than ten years serving with three different companies as a chief financial officer and with one company as a chief information officer. His specialty has been mentoring, starting, and developing early-stage businesses and advising or leading them through the first to third stages of equity and debt capital investment. This has involved activities in numerous domestic and international companies, projects, and settings where he has enjoyed working with associates in joint problem-solving for companies, states, and countries throughout the world.

Clark and his sweetheart, Leah, have a blended family of ten children and thirteen grandchildren who they deeply treasure. They reside near Salt Lake City, Utah, in the foothills of those mountains in which they, still today, love to hike and mountain bike.

Scan to visit

https://www.facebook.com/clarkrburbidge/

https://www.facebook.com/blendedfamilyproject/